REENGINEERING
THE FACTORY

Also available from ASQC Quality Press

A TQM Approach to Achieving Manufacturing Excellence
A. Richard Shores

Survival of the Fittest: Total Quality Control and Management Evolution
A. Richard Shores

Reengineering the Organization: A Step-by-Step Approach to Corporate Revitalization
Jeffrey N. Lowenthal

Process Reengineering: The Key to Achieving Breakthrough Success
Lon Roberts

Management by Policy: How Companies Focus Their Total Quality Efforts to Achieve Competitive Advantage
Brendan Collins and Ernest Huge

Quality Function Deployment: Linking a Company with Its Customers
Ronald G. Day

To request a complimentary catalog of publications, call 800-248-1946.

REENGINEERING THE FACTORY

A Primer for World-Class Manufacturing

A. Richard Shores

ASQC Quality Press
Milwaukee, Wisconsin

REENGINEERING THE FACTORY:
A PRIMER FOR WORLD-CLASS MANUFACTURING
A. Richard Shores

Library of Congress Cataloging-in-Publication Data
Shores, A. Richard
    Reengineering the factory: a primer for world-class manufacturing/
A. Richard Shores.
        p.   cm.
        Includes bibliographical references and index.
        ISBN 0-87389-249-6
        1. Production management—Quality control.   2. Total quality
management.   3. Computer integrated manufacturing systems.
I. Title.
TS156.S494   1994
658.5—dc20   93-41650
                                                                            CIP

10 9 8 7 6 5 4 3 2 1

ISBN 0-87389-249-6

Acquisitions Editor: Susan Westergard
Project Editor: Kelley Cardinal
Production Editor: Annette Wall
Marketing Administrator: Mark Olson
Set in Avant Garde and Galliard by Linda J. Shepherd.
Cover design by Daryl Poulin.
Printed and bound by BookCrafters, Inc.

ASQC Mission: To facilitate continuous improvement and increase customer
satisfaction by identifying, communicating, and promoting the use of quality
principles, concepts, and technologies; and thereby be recognized throughout
the world as the leading authority on, and champion for, quality.

For a free copy of the ASQC Quality Press Publications Catalog, including
ASQC membership information, call 800-248-1946.

Printed in the United States of America

    Printed on acid-free recycled paper

   ASQC
     Quality Press
     611 East Wisconsin Avenue
     Milwaukee, Wisconsin 53202

CONTENTS

FOREWORD

U.S. manufacturing has been a great success story over much of the last half decade. After suffering through negligible productivity growth rates and some highly publicized losses in market share, American manufacturers have engineered a real turnaround. Recent productivity gains have exceeded the long-term averages, and export growth has become one of the nation's economic highlights.

Analysts point to two main forces at work that have caused this impressive result. The first is the usual competitive reaction to challenging economic times, namely, to slash costs, downsize, and vigorously outsource functions that are not core competencies. While these short-term improvements are real, the concern is that they are onetime gains that will not be sustainable in the longer term. The next economic cycle or a realignment of exchange rates will put these companies back on the underperformer list.

A group of leading companies has taken a second, different approach. They have made a long-term commitment to total quality management. That means viewing every part of their business as a process that can be analyzed and systematically improved, using recently developed but proven practices as detailed in this book. These companies have achieved gains that will actually continue to improve over time. In addition, they have created a different kind of workforce that is highly trained, self-motivated, and prepared to carry the enterprise to new levels of competition in the future.

And there will certainly be new levels. Agile manufacturing, or networked virtual manufacturing, is seen by many as the next wave of manufacturing. It's also a way for U.S. manufacturers to regain and assert world leadership over the next decade or two. Electronic commerce, using the wide bandwidth of the digital information infrastructure now coming into place, gives companies a way to put together teams for fast response and low cost. These new approaches will be a natural extension to the world-class manufacturing practices put in place by today's leading companies.

What's the difference between just downsizing for short-term gains and real productivity improvement for the long term? *Reengineering the Factory* provides a simplified overview, in layperson's terms, of what it takes to win in today's manufacturing marketplace. To illustrate the extraordinary gains that can be achieved, chapter 15 details the $125M company that reduced warranty and material costs by $2M each, did not have $15M in inventory sitting around to make up for defects during production, cut overhead by 60 percent using self-managed teams, and more.

There is no magic. The techniques are well known, but that does not mean the journey to lasting improvement is an easy one. First comes top management commitment, and that often is the hardest part because it's a multiyear project. But successfully completed, reengineering can put your company on a new competitive level. Those who embark on the journey should be prepared to learn new skills, such as process improvement, and to exercise new management practices, such as change management. Changing an organization's culture is management's hardest job, but the rewards are most satisfying. I wish you well as you start down the road to world-class manufacturing.

John Young
Retired President and CEO, Hewlett-Packard

PREFACE

This book is a primer on world-class manufacturing (WCM) methods. It is written for individuals who desire to learn how to achieve WCM through the reengineering process. Reengineering is a process of renewal, using new technologies and methods to achieve better performance and customer satisfaction.

The material in this book was originally intended as a training tool, a conceptual introduction to reengineering methods and WCM for the employees of a U.S. automobile manufacturing company. It has been subsequently modified and expanded to its present form.

There are four themes to be discussed in this text.

1. World-class manufacturing status is achieved not by doing one thing well, but by investment and application of several interrelated breakthrough manufacturing technologies. Eight of these WCM technologies are explained in terms of the benefits provided to quality, productivity, and flexibility.

2. The benefits of WCM technologies do not end with implementation. Continuous improvement methods (kaizen) must be applied to every method with unending enthusiasm. Continuous improvement methods are explained for each of the eight WCM methods discussed.

3. The eight WCM methods are interrelated in a logical framework that functions as a management system. Three total

quality management systems are discussed in terms of their relative strengths.

4. An implementation guide, based on the author's experience, is included in chapter 15.

This book is intended as a comprehensive introduction to the principles of WCM. Many relational diagrams are used to explain the interrelationships and dynamics of WCM methods.

INTRODUCTION: ECONOMIC GROWTH MODEL

Most economists agree that the U.S. economy is suffering because productivity has not grown enough during the last 10 to 15 years. During the 1980s, nations such as Japan and West Germany consistently outpaced our productivity growth and, subsequently, made huge inroads into many of our traditional markets—domestic as well as international.

The Japanese led this economic attack by revolutionizing their approach to manufacturing. Total quality control (TQC), just-in-time (JIT) production, and quality function deployment (QFD) are examples of new manufacturing methods employed by the Japanese to improve quality, productivity, and flexibility. By employing these new manufacturing technologies, they have established higher customer expectations and have thereby set new standards for world-class manufacturing performance.

A few U.S. manufacturers have demonstrated the ability to use these methods effectively and have made economic comebacks. At the same time, others have tried to copy these methods and failed. In some cases, failure can be attributed to trying to do too little too late. For others, it may be because management tried to do too much too fast. In either case, the lesson to be learned is that these tools alone do not guarantee success. They must be tuned and selectively applied based on the individual needs of a business and its environment. Success with these tools depends solely on the knowledge, judgment, and commitment of the local management team.

On a broader scale, national productivity depends on the success of many businesses and industries. This requires that world-class manufacturing methods be used successfully throughout industry before our national productivity can show the kind of growth required to sustain real improvements in the standard of living. This point is illustrated in Figure I.1, which is supported by the following explanation.

Objective. The objective for the economy should be continuous economic growth. This is defined as growth in gross national product and real income. For a business, economic growth is defined as increases in sales and profit. A national economy, which is composed of many businesses, is dependent on the growth of those businesses.

Strategy. The strategy for this growth is world-class manufacturing. Our manufacturing operations must be superior to our competitors' in the ability to satisfy customers. *Totally satisfied customers* means that their desires and expectations are always met without disappointment.

Goal. The goal for WCM is total customer satisfaction, which is achieved by providing superior products, superior value, and superior availability. If customers find your products superior to your competitors' products, they will buy from you.

Tactics. The tactics for arriving at the goal of total customer satisfaction relate to achieving superiority in quality, productivity and flexibility. Superior quality means products and services that are superior in what are sometimes referred to as the FURPS attributes (functionality, usability, reliability, performance, supportability/serviceability). Superior productivity means that all resources are used more efficiently, with the least amount of waste. Included in the resource set are people, material, equipment, and information. Superior flexibility means that the business has shorter delivery time, greater responsiveness to changing customer needs, and the ability to produce various customized products without a cost penalty.

Processes. The processes are the specific activities used to integrate the resources of the business such that value is created in a superior manner. These processes include, but are not limited to, the following main activities.

- Understanding customer expectations and desires
- Creating product and process specifications that meet customer desires
- Designing products that are superior in meeting customer desires
- Investing in the resources required to implement the processes and achieve high productivity
- Understanding and planning for customer desires as they relate to volumes, responsiveness, and variety

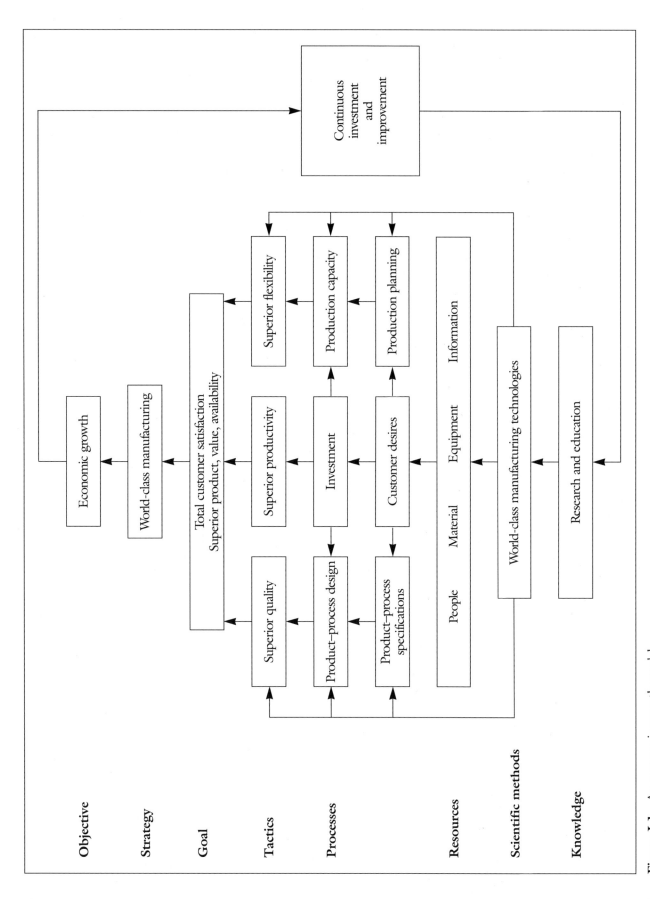

Figure I.1. An economic growth model.

- Establishing the correct level of production capacity for achieving customer desires

Resources. The resources are the people, material, equipment, and information used in the processes to achieve superiority.

Scientific methods. There are eight world-class manufacturing technologies to be applied when reengineering the factory. They are used to manage and improve the resources and processes toward higher levels of customer satisfaction. These are defined in the discussion of Figure I.2.

Knowledge. Knowledge is the net gain of continuing research and education. By definition, improvements in WCM technologies are derived from new knowledge gained through the research and education of the people in the business.

Continuous investment and improvement. Continuous growth of the economy is achieved when the pieces of the model are integrated over time. Revenues are derived from economic growth and must be applied to increasing research and education. Better technologies and methods will come from this investment and thus provide for continuous economic growth.

Traditional manufacturing methods have evolved over the years through individual ingenuity, sociology, and trial and error. The evolutionary effect has been that each new idea is tried on a small scale and slowly becomes accepted and layered on top of and parallel to other, outdated methods. The result is a suboptimum factory design, ill-suited to the needs of the present-day competitive environment.

Reengineering concepts presume that it is possible to draw a line between present world-class methods and older, less effective methods. Given that it is possible to define the best of the best methods, the challenge in reengineering the factory is to integrate and optimize these methods into a comprehensive system of implementation.

The eight tools illustrated in Figure I.2 are representative of the best technologies available to the manufacturing industry today. They are the subject of discussion in two contexts: (1) What are the eight tools and what contribution do they make to improving the factory? and (2) How are the eight tools interrelated and how do they integrate within the framework of the management system?

SUMMARY

The U.S. manufacturing industry has made limited progress in applying world-class manufacturing tools. Some businesses have experienced phenomenal success. Others have tried and not done so well. Failure on the part of a few should not be a deterrent to top management to understand and apply these tools. Rather, failure

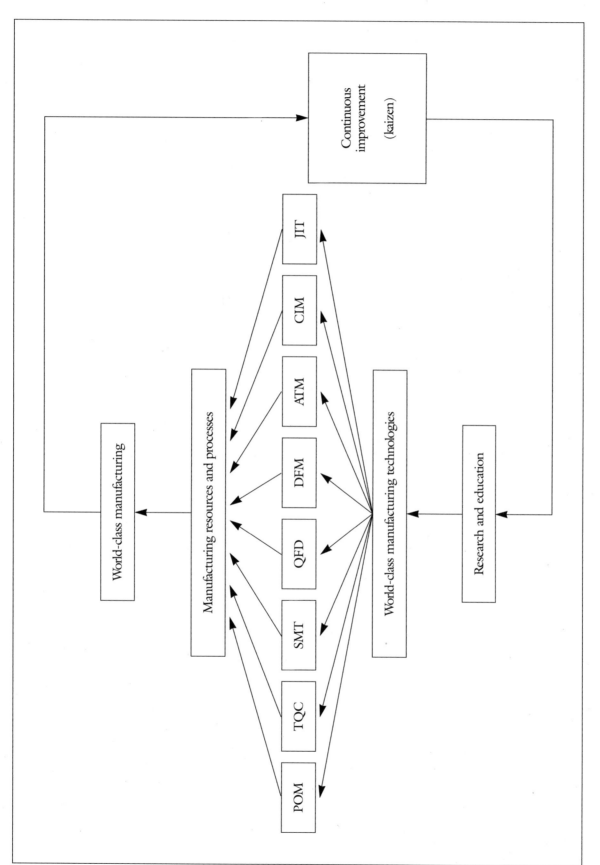

Figure I.2. WCM technologies in the economic growth model. Key: kaizen, continuous improvement; POM, process of management; TQC, total quality control; SMT, self-managed teams; QFD, quality function deployment; DFM, design for manufacturing; ATM, automation; CIM, computer-integrated manufacturing; JIT, just-in-time.

should serve as a reason to modify the approach. Every business and its environment are different, and improvements are constantly being made to the tools. Management must stay abreast of these changes.

The economic growth model described here is intentionally simple. One business does not make an economy and one tool does not make a WCM strategy. Every business has a responsibility to its employees and the economy to be successful. Every manager has a responsibility to the business to help it succeed. Management must therefore be committed to evaluating these WCM tools, modifying them to fit a situation, and continuously improving them.

TOTAL QUALITY MANAGEMENT

The root of reengineering concepts is total quality management (TQM), a term to which many people still adhere. When TQM is defined in an all-encompassing process improvement system (as it should be), it serves the purposes of reengineering very well. Does that make reengineering a new buzzword? Maybe, but the proponents of reengineering like to point out that the semantics of reengineering more strongly emphasize the need for radical redesign and change, whereas TQM seems to be biased toward gradual change and improvement. Reengineering should be thought of at the conceptual level as a process of renewal for the business. TQM should be considered as a framework or management system for implementing the reengineering process and integrating world-class manufacturing tools. This concept will be discussed further in chapters 11–14.

TQM can be defined as follows:

Total: The sum of all elements of the business

Quality: The desired state of accuracy, variation, or acceptance of all products and services of the business

Management: The methods and actions employed to achieve the desired outcome

In a TQM environment, the scientific methods selected for use make explicit contributions to the effectiveness of the business' resources, processes, and tactics. Tables 1.1, 1.2, and 1.3 describe the contributions that the eight world-class manufacturing technologies make toward improving the effectiveness of the business resources, processes, and tactics, respectively.

Table 1.1. The effects of WCM technologies on resources.

World-class manufacturing technologies

Resources	POM	TQC	SMT	QFD	DFM	ATM	CIM	JIT
People	Establish a team culture that supports continuous improvement of customer satisfaction.	People work in quality circles (QCs) to improve the quality/cost and delivery of processes.	People work in teams to make decisions about the operation and improvement of their processes.	Cross-functional teams work together to specify and design products, materials, and process requirements.	Cross-functional teams work (concurrently) together to design products for best quality and lowest cost.	People use automated machinery to improve the speed and quality of their process.	People use automatic storage, retrieval, and transfer of information to operate and improve processes.	People are flexible in skills and time to be able to work when and where needed.
Material	Relationships with suppliers ensure a continuous improvement in quality, cost, and delivery (JIT delivery).	Material is received defect free and QCs work with suppliers to continuously reduce problems.	SMTs work with each other and suppliers to make decisions about sourcing, spec changes, and improvements.	The Taguchi quality loss function is used to improve quality and reduce cost of quality.	The number of parts and part numbers are minimized, as are the number of suppliers.	Material handlers use carousels, conveyors, and other equipment to minimize handling of materials.	Materials specifications, inventory, and cost are stored on electronic data bases and are accessible throughout the factory.	Material is pulled and received in the quantities needed at the time needed as signaled by a card (kanban).
Equipment	Equipment is purchased and maintained as required to meet goals.	Equipment performance is continuously monitored and maintained with operating specs. Total productive maintenance (TPM).	SMTs work together to analyze equipment performance, maintain it, and make improvements (TPM).	The Taguchi quality loss function is used to improve quality and reduce cost of quality.	Products are designed for assembly (DFA) using the best quality, lowest cost equipment.	New machinery, robotics, and other forms of equipment are used where quality, cost, and flexibility are improved.	Work instructions for operators and equipment are stored on electronic data bases and available throughout the factory.	Equipment is flexible and available without bottlenecks to perform tasks with minimum queues. Stops for quality problems (jidoka).
Information	Management shares all information with employees to enable them to participate in decisions.	People use SQC tools to analyze information about processes to continuously improve them.	SMTs make all decisions about cost, quality, and delivery. They have access to the necessary management information.	The Taguchi quality loss function is used to improve quality and reduce cost of quality.	Designers have all information about processes, equipment, defect and cost rates.	Machinery and people have direct access to instructions as required to perform tasks.	Information about quality, cost, orders, delivery, and design is readily available anywhere in the factory (LAN).	JIT is a work orderless environment and scheduling information is based on throughput and cycle time.

Table 1.2. The effects of WCM technologies on processes.

World-class manufacturing technologies

Processes	POM	TQC	SMT	QFD	DFM	ATM	CIM	JIT
Continuous improvement (kaizen)	The Deming cycle is used to continuously improve the effectiveness of all processes and world-class manufacturing technologies. (Plan / Do / Check / Act)							
Understand customer desires	Customer needs and expectations are the primary focus of the business and product plan (hoshin).	SQC tools are used to analyze customer designs (new seven tools, seven tools).	Marketing and design teams meet with customers and review benchmark info about customers.	Cross-functional teams (SMTs) use the voice of the customer to set customer specifications.	Cross-functional teams analyze customer needs for cost.	Automated systems can be used to collect and sort customer and competitive data.	Customer information can be linked to anywhere in the factory through local area networks (LANs).	Understand customer delivery requirements.
Create product and process specifications	Structured methods (QFD) are used to analyze customer needs and translate into specifications and plans (hoshin).	SQC tools are used to prioritize and establish limits on specifications (new seven tools, seven tools).	Marketing, design, and manufacturing teams work together to select specifications.	Teams use the house of quality to define the product and process plans.	Process and supplier capabilities are analyzed for cost and quality.	Automated systems can be used to analyze and recommend specifications.	Process and supplier capability can be linked by LAN and EDI.	Establish responsiveness times, maximum allowable delivery, cycle times, and inventory queues.
Design product and processes	Cross-functional teams, new seven tools) are used to design products that fit processes, and processes that meet product and customer desires (DFM).	The product objectives are stated in a plan (hoshin). Design analysis is done along the way to ensure quality (DOE).	Design and manufacturing teams design products and processes.	Teams use design of experiments (DOE) and other analysis to design a *robust product*.	Concurrent engineering is used to simultaneously design products, processes, and parts for lowest cost.	Computer-aided design/engineering (CAD/CAE) tools can improve the quality and productivity of design.	Use common or neutral format data base to move design and process information between design and manufacturing.	Plan routings, restocking signals, and stocking locations for all parts and products.
Understand production demand	Structured analysis tools (QFD, new seven tools) are used to understand volume, quality, flexibility, and cost requirements of production plans (hoshin).	Product forecasts and orders are statistically analyzed to *Plan* demand (seven tools).	Production and marketing teams analyze orders and forecast to plan demand.	Teams use statistical tools to do production planning.	Volume and variety must be understood for DFM.	Computer-aided tools can be used to analyze orders and plan production requirements (MPS/MRP).	Marketing order systems are linked to MPS/MRP for production planning.	Uses build-to-order (BTO) and kanban to pull requirements along without scheduling the product flow.
Make investments	Training and capital are provided to ensure that the business is capable of meeting its goals and continuously improving.	The project hoshin and demand are analyzed to make investment decisions; *Do* (seven tools).	The teams work in an MBO fashion from project objectives and demand to make decisions.	Teams make investments according to process and production plan.	Investments are made according to plan.	All investments in automation should be based on ROI for cost, quality, and flexibility.	Invest in networks, servers, and disk drives based on ROI.	Invest in kanban bins, barcode, and inventory as required.
Maximize production capacity	Proper incentives are provided and reviews of the business are conducted to identify areas of underutilization, bottlenecks, or attitude problems that affect productivity.	Production cost, quality, and delivery are analyzed to verify and/or improve results; *Check act* (seven tools).	The teams are accountable to verify results and take corrective action.	Quality loss function is used to check results and improve utilization.	Feedback is provided to engineers on how well product fits process.	Utilize automation fully by minimizing downtime and setup time (TPM).	The availability of timely, accurate information improves capacity.	Review queues and cycle times to ensure there are no bottlenecks.

Table 1.3. The effects of WCM technologies on tactics.

World-class manufacturing technologies

Tactics	POM	TQC	SMT	QFD	DFM	ATM	CIM	JIT
Quality • Information • Equipment • People • Product design • Material	Improving the quality of management creates a quality environment.	Continuous improvement of quality (COQ) processes and inputs.	People working as a team solve more problems than individuals can.	A more precise understanding of customer needs improves quality of product.	Products should be designed to use best quality processes and materials.	Simplification before automation improves quality. ATM is more consistent.	Electronic data transfer improves quality.	Eliminating inventory queues imposes a do-it-right-the-first-time attitude. Line is stopped by problems (jadoka).
Productivity • Cost of quality • Asset utilization • Efficiency • Waste • Rework	A quality environment and a good management system is a productive environment.	Reduces COQ and improves efficiency by elimination of waste and rework.	Decisions made at the lowest level eliminate bureaucracy and hierarchy.	A more precise definition of product design eliminates design rework and improves productivity.	Products should be designed to require least amount of labor, material and overhead.	ATM becomes more productive as technology improves and wages increase.	Improving the quality of information improves productivity.	Low inventory queues improve asset utilization and require short setups without bottlenecks.
Flexibility • Timeliness • Cycle time • Responsiveness • Variety • Customization	A good management system is responsive to changes in the environment.	Efficient processes have low cycle times and better timeliness.	The elimination of bureaucracy and hierarchy improves cycle time and responsiveness.	The elimination of design rework improves time to market and timeliness of new products.	Products should be designed to fit a short cycle time and flexible manufacturing environment.	Electronic storage and retrieval of information enables ATM to provide short cycle times.	Electronic storage and transfer of information is fast, timely, and flexible.	Low inventory queues, short setups, and no bottlenecks improve cycle time, responsiveness, and ability to produce variety.

Tables 1.1, 1.2, and 1.3 provide an overview of the way world-class manufacturing methods influence the success and continued growth and improvement of the business. A new employee or an employee new to the ideas of TQM might use these tables as ready reference and as a reminder of why these methods are utilized. Each of these methods will be discussed in more detail in the following chapters.

SUMMARY

TQM should be thought of as the management system for implementing the process of reengineering the factory through the integration of WCM tools. The focus is on continuous and sometimes radical improvement in the way a business meets customer needs and responds to its changing environment.

The eight WCM tools may individually or collectively represent radical change for the business. The effects on the business are widespread, impacting the people, processes, strategies, and customers as defined in Tables 1.1–1.3.

KAIZEN—CONTINUOUS IMPROVEMENT

Kaizen (pronounced ky'zen) is the Japanese term for *gradual, unending improvement,* writes Masaaki Imai in his book *Kaizen* (Imai 1986). Kaizen is a fundamental philosophy of Japanese manufacturers. It is the driving force for TQC, QFD, JIT, and the other elements of world-class manufacturing. All new methods are evaluated by the contribution they make to the speed and efficiency of improving the business toward its objective of economic growth through customer satisfaction. It is stated that everything in the business is a process, and that all processes must be improved following the principles of kaizen. This includes doing little things better, and setting ever higher goals for improvement.

Kaizen is an integral part of TQC known as USA–PDCA (plan, do, check, and act). Together kaizen and TQC provide for a process of continuous improvement of everything in the business. This concept is illustrated in Figure 2.1. The TQC/kaizen improvement methodology is used as a framework to show how each of the scientific methods can be used to continuously improve the business. In subsequent pages, the eight scientific methods are discussed in terms of the issues and actions required at each stage of the improvement cycle, along with the tools and training relevant to that particular method. It should be noted that the utilization of any one of these WCM methods is capable of providing breakthrough improvements in quality, productivity, or delivery. As each method is applied, there is a further opportunity to improve the results derived from its use.

World-class manufacturing technologies

Total quality control	Issues and actions	Tools	Training
Improve quality, cost, flexibility (Continuous improvement [kaizen])			
Form the team — *Understand*	–Identify the responsible people for the activities in question.	–Quality circles	All employees –Work in groups –Design and interpret surveys –Math for SPC –Satisfy customers –Write issue statements –Use USA–PDCA –Construct flowcharts –Develop process quality measures –Cause-and-effect diagrams (fishbone charts) –How to collect data –Seven SPC tools –New seven tools –Manage time
Understand the situation	–Who are the customers? –What is the product? –What are customer expectations? –Are the expectations met?	–Data/spec sheets –Customer surveys –Benchmarking –Seven SPC tools	
Select an issue — *Select an issue*	–Which issue is most important and most in need of improvement? –Which process is responsible?	–Seven SQC tools –Pareto chart	
Analyze the process — *Analyze*	–How does the process work? –What is the level of performance? –What are potential causes? –What are actual causes?	–Flowcharts –Seven SPC tools –Fishbone chart –New seven tools –WCM methods	
Plan a change — *Plan*	–Devise a plan to improve metric (process performance measure/process quality measure). –Design an experiment.	–New seven tools –Design of experiments –Potential problem analysis	Engineers –Taguchi design of experiments
Implement the plan — *Do*	–Implement the experiment or plan.		
Verify the results — *Check*	–Check the results of the change	–Seven SPC tools –Customer surveys	Supervisors –Team facilitation –Hoshin
Make routine — *Act*	–Document the change and make it routine or change the plan. –Move to next opportunity.	–Poka yoke –Tooling –Production engineering changes –Kaizen	

Figure 2.1. Kaizen and the TQC improvement cycle.

THE IMPROVEMENT CYCLE

Each stage of the improvement cycle is shown in the flowchart in Figure 2.1 and is defined as follows:

Form the team. All WCM businesses have found that employees are more productive when working as a team. The Japanese have emphasized the benefits of quality circles and, more recently, U.S. manufacturers are learning the benefits of self-managed teams (SMT). The process improvement methodology, therefore, begins with the formation and training of the team that is responsible for the product, service, or process to be considered.

Understand the situation. The first step in this process is to understand who your customer is and what products are needed. The Team must understand the answers to the questions posed in the *issues and actions* column of Figure 2.1.

Select an issue. After the issues are thoroughly understood, the team must select the issue that is in most need of improvement.

Analyze the process. After the issue is identified, the process must be analyzed to determine the cause of the deviation in performance.

Plan a change. The team must plan to change the process in some way to correct the deficiency in performance.

Implement the plan. This may involve conducting an experiment or making an outright change in the process, depending on the risk.

Verify the results. Data is taken to verify that the planned changes actually improved the situation.

Make routine. After the changes have been verified, they are documented as production change orders and/or tooling is designed to make the new process routine and foolproof for the operators.

The team then moves to the next largest opportunity for improvement and works through the same steps again to complete the cycle in the practice of kaizen.

Most successful implementations of kaizen use some sort of a review mechanism for the team. The improvement cycle is very often portrayed on a storyboard, which is a picture of the steps followed during the improvement cycle. Teams can display these boards in their work areas and use them when making presentations.

TOOLS

Each WCM method has a unique set of tools associated with its implementation. At the same time, there are many tools shared by the eight WCM methods. The common tools relate to the continuous improvement methodology of the TQC/kaizen framework as shown in Figure 2.1.

TRAINING

The fact that there are many common tools has value to the training process. Employees can be trained in the basics of TQC and have most of what they need to be successful in learning and applying the other methods. More information on the structure of training appears in chapter 12.

SUMMARY

The concept of kaizen is an old and established philosophy of continuous improvement. There are no secrets to understanding this philosophy. It is analytical and rigorous. The focus is on a constant repetition of identification of issues, analysis of causes, and implementation of planned solutions.

The USA–PDCA method is just one approach to this analytical process. It is a simple enhancement of the Deming wheel (Deming 1982), and is used by companies around the world. The characteristics of this method are that it is simple and easy to teach, implies simple and straightforward questions about the process, and is easily adaptable to review and application to a storyboard.

TOTAL QUALITY CONTROL

Total quality control (TQC) is now accepted by most people in business as an essential part of achieving customer satisfaction and competitive success. This was not the case in 1980, when TQC was still a buzzword. At that time, most Americans viewed TQC at a very superficial level. They saw Japanese TQC limited to quality circles, statistical process/quality control (SPC/SQC) and the process improvement methodology described in chapter 2 as kaizen, and sometimes known as the Deming wheel. These methods were combined to achieve customer satisfaction through the continuous improvement of all processes, and are often referred to by the Japanese as companywide quality control (CWQC).

For the most part, the concepts of TQC, or CWQC, originated in the United States. They were born in the minds of W. Edwards Deming, J. M. Juran, and Armand V. Feigenbaum (Feigenbaum introduced the term *total quality control* in his book *Total Quality Control*, published in 1951). Japanese businesses adopted these principles following World War II as part of the effort to rebuild the Japanese economy. At that time, Japanese products had a reputation for being cheap and of poor quality. Japan needed to overcome that reputation in order to build a strong export economy. Deming and Juran, among others, were asked to consult with the Japanese and teach them how to design and build good quality products at competitive prices.

The Japanese have achieved a great deal by applying TQC principles. They have made huge inroads into U.S. automobile markets, as well as steel, consumer electronics, tooling, and many other areas by improving quality, productivity, and flexibility through TQC.

Some American companies are starting to be successful in applying these same techniques, but they still have a long way to go. There is a long organizational learning period required to make TQC a way of life, and the Japanese have a 25-year head start. Most American companies have been practicing TQC for less than 10 years, and fewer than 5 percent can boast the achievements of the average Japanese company today. U.S. understanding of TQC has progressed considerably since 1980. Today, it is broader and more comprehensive, thanks to a huge outpouring of literature from both Japan and the United States. The knowledge of TQC is widespread among quality managers, and through company, industry, and consulting training programs are becoming more generally understood and accepted by other employees. If TQC is to become a way of life here, as it is in Japan, then every employee—production worker, engineer, administrator, and manager—must fully understand and use the principles of TQC, some of which are described in the following sections.

CUSTOMER SATISFACTION

It is often quoted that customers are the primary reason for being in business and that the revenues they provide are the lifeblood of the business. For this reason, the Japanese and other world-class manufacturers treat customer satisfaction as their fundamental objective.

Achieving customer satisfaction means meeting or surpassing customers' expectations. Restated, it means providing a product or service without disappointments. Most people can remember at least one experience when they received something new, perhaps something they had made great sacrifice to purchase, only to find it defective or otherwise short of expectations. It does not take many disappointed customers before word gets around and the business starts to suffer.

As stated earlier, the key measures of customer satisfaction relate to the quality, productivity, and flexibility of the business. The goals of TQC are to consistently improve the process measures toward higher levels of customer satisfaction.

QUALITY CIRCLES

Quality circles (QCs) grew out of the early 1960s in Japan as a result of the Japanese focus on quality. The actual roots of QCs are elusive, but many people believe that QCs began from a traditional aspect of Japanese management. Japanese supervisors are noted for bringing their employees into a circle before every shift to talk about the daily plans and potential problems. As quality improvement became the focus of these meetings, they became known as quality circles. Subsequently, quality circles have become formalized and a regular part of Japanese TQC practice.

HOSHIN

Hoshin is a Japanese term translated to mean *policy deployment*. The Japanese use hoshin as a planning and review tool within the TQC methodology. Each year, the president of the company sets key objectives and strategies (hoshins) and presents them to his or her subordinates. These hoshins are reviewed until understanding and consensus are achieved. The subordinates then develop their departmental goals and strategies relative to the president's hoshins. This process is continued through the hierarchy until the hoshins (policies) are deployed throughout the business.

Hoshin is a rigorous process, requiring accurate documentation of objectives, measures, strategies, limits of deviations, and regular reviews of results. The company president uses hoshin as the basis for his or her annual review.

Some Japanese say that the hoshin process was developed from management by objectives (MBO), which they learned from the United States. The Japanese enhanced MBO by encapsulating it with the PDCA methodology (Shores 1988).

STATISTICAL PROCESS/ QUALITY CONTROL

Statistical process/quality control (SPC/SQC) is the application of statistical tools to the analysis of process deviation. The science of statistics is the study of variation. In the quality control environment, statistics are used to separate random variation from nonrandom variation. Nonrandom variation has an assignable cause that can be traced and remedied, while random variation does not. It is important for people to understand what type of variation they are dealing with; otherwise, they will waste considerable time and effort chasing problems over which they have no control. SPC/SQC is a fundamental tool of TQC.

SEVEN TOOLS

The *seven tools* are the most common statistical tools used in SQC. They were popularized by Dr. Kaoru Ishikawa (Ishikawa 1982). They represent the simplest approach to teaching nontechnical employees the use of SQC principles to manage their process.

1. *Cause-and-effect diagram:* A fishbone-type chart used to dissect the possible and probable causes to a problem

2. *Pareto chart:* A bar graph used to show data sorted from largest to smallest

3. *Histogram:* A chart used to show the percentage of data distributed over time or another horizontal axis

4. *Control chart:* A chart used to show data plotted over time with statistical control limits calculated, and to show that the process is operating within statistical control limits

5. *Bar graph:* A chart used to quantitatively compare data by exhibiting the data size or quantity as the length of the bar

6. *Check sheet:* A simple sheet used to record the number of samples and defects found during inspection

7. *Scatter diagram:* A chart that shows data plotted as points within two axes, used to do regression analysis and to understand relationships of different data

NEW SEVEN TOOLS

The *new seven tools* were popularized by Shigeru Mizuno of Japan, in a book entitled *Management for Quality Improvement* (Mizuno 1986). The new seven tools are generally considered to be management tools to improve the planning and strategy of the business, and are typically thought of in reference to TQC and TQM. They are described as follows:

1. *The relations diagram:* A technique used to clarify causal relationships in a complex problem in order to find a solution.

2. *The KJ method (affinity diagram):* A participative method of collating diverse sets of information about a problem and sorting the information into categories, thus showing the affinity of one piece of information to another.

3. *Systematic diagram:* A method for finding suitable techniques for achieving stated objectives by breaking them down into component parts, thus simplifying the task. The result enables workers to see the entire task at a glance.

4. *Matrix diagram:* A diagram much like the structured planning method referred to as hoshin. The primary objective(s) is (are) shown on one axis, and specific strategies and/or problems that might be encountered are shown on the other axis. It enables the manager to see at a glance the relationships of objectives, strategies, and potential problems.

5. *Matrix data analysis:* A method of arranging data in a matrix diagram so that a large array of data can be comprehended easily.

6. *Process decision program chart (PDPC):* A method that helps one determine which processes to use by evaluating the progress of events and the variety of eventual outcomes.

7. *Arrow diagram:* A Pert chart or similar diagram using arrows to show the sequence of events to plan a daily schedule and monitor results.

POKA YOKE

Poka yoke is a Japanese term meaning that solutions to problems and deviations in the process should be foolproof. The process, and the remedies to process problems, should be so foolproof, through tooling or other mechanisms, that the problems will not recur in the future. Poka yoke is a common TQC tool.

SUMMARY

Total quality control was the first glimpse of a new manufacturing era coming out of Japan. While many companies in the United States were aware of the teachings of W. Edwards Deming and J. M. Juran, they paid little heed to them until the the 1970s when the Japanese began to tout their successes. By the early 1980s, American companies were clamoring for more knowledge about TQC, and many visited Japan in search of the source of all this newfound wisdom.

As American companies tried to copy the Japanese, many ran into problems and backed away from their efforts. In particular, quality circles seemed to be the most difficult concept to copy and they received considerable bad press in the United States. By the late 1980s, different forms of employee involvement became popular in the United States. QCs, deemed too oriented to Japanese culture, were replaced with self-directed work teams and other team-oriented structures.

Although some aspects of TQC are not favored in the United States, it is still the predominant WCM tool practiced by U.S. companies in their quest for excellence. It has evolved into many forms, including TQM and ISO 9000, and is an important element of the Malcolm Baldrige National Quality Award (MBNQA).

PROCESS OF MANAGEMENT

Management, viewed as a process by many people, involves a methodical approach to setting the direction of the business. One example of this is at the Hewlett-Packard company, where managers are trained in the *process of management* (POM). The POM is based on research of the management practices of over 150 successful managers in the Hewlett-Packard company. The steps in the POM model are

1. Establish a purpose and direction

2. Build a shared vision

3. Develop shared plans

4. Lead the course of action

5. Evaluate the results and process

6. Continuously improve the result and process

The *process of management* suggests that TQC principles can be used to improve management, just as in any other process. If managers are trained in the management process, and TQC is applied to improve the quality of the process, then the quality of the collective management system can be improved. The improvement cycle applying to POM is shown in Figure 4.1.

Improving the quality of management means that wasted time and resources are reduced. All people, managers and nonmanagers alike, spend less time figuring out what to do, and less time doing the wrong things. In a TQM environment, the whole organization is focused around a common set of goals with a mutually rewarding outcome; bottlenecks, wheel spinning, cross-motivations, and tangential thinking are continuously reduced until eliminated.

World-class manufacturing technologies

Process of management	Issues and actions	Tools	Training
Improve quality, cost, flexibility			All employees
Form the team — *Understand*	–Teams and linkages are formed across organization.	–Self-managed teams	–Define organizational relationships
Understand the situation	–Internal and external customers' needs and expectations are identified. –Management functions are identified. –Management performance is reviewed.	–Organization chart –Flowcharts –In-out charts –Customer survey –Employee survey	–Understand customer–supplier relationships –All TQC tools training –All SMT training –Process of management (POM)
Select an issue — *Select an issue*	–Opportunities for improvement are identified. –Management issues are prioritized and selected.	–Annual reviews –Seven SPC tools	–Functions of TPM model –Hoshin training –Conducting effective reviews
Analyze the process — *Analyze*	–How is management function provided? –Which management tools are used? –Are there more effective tools?	–TQM model –WCM methods	
Plan a change — *Plan*	–Vision and objectives are established. –Measures and strategy are set.	–Leadership tools (hoshin)	Engineers –QFD—house of quality
Implement the plan — *Do*	–Commit the resources. –Provide the incentives.	–People, equipment, training –Salary, benefits, and gain sharing	
Verify the results — *Check*	–Regular reviews.	–Employee survey –Customer survey –Business results	
Make routine — *Act*	–Make change permanent or change plan. –Move to next opportunity.	–Training –Documentation –Kaizen	
Continuous improvement (kaizen)			

Figure 4.1. POM and the improvement cycle.

In order to improve the quality of management, managers must continuously review the effectiveness of their decisions in each of these elements and make changes to improve them, which means they need some form of assessment tool to periodically achieve a broad understanding of how the organization, people, and processes are responding. The assessment can be done by monitoring process measures when available, and by surveying employees and customers. For example, time to market, return on investment, or market share might be good measures for the product definition process. However, they may not be true measures of market potential, which may only unveil itself through customer surveys. Employee turnover rate might be a good measure of employee satisfaction; but, depending on the company and the economy, an employee survey may be the only way to get a valid answer. It is important for every manager to remember that employees are customers of the management system, and that their needs must be considered along with the needs of the external customer.

In the Hewlett-Packard POM class, for example, each manager sends out a survey to his or her employees asking them to rate the manager in the specified management categories. These scores are used as a benchmark for each manager, and are considered as opportunities for future improvement during the class. After the class, follow-up surveys are conducted to test the improvements achieved by the managers. These scores are kept confidential and are not used as part of a manager's ranking system. However, the scores can be aggregated and the overall managerial ability and improvement of the organization can be measured over time.

The Hewlett-Packard company also conducts an annual employee survey that is designed to reveal employee attitudes about a broader spectrum of issues. This survey includes questions about morale, pay, plans, teamwork, customer satisfaction, and several other categories. A considerable amount of statistical analysis is done on the survey results to identify strengths, weaknesses, and trends. This information is then used by Hewlett-Packard management to plan for future improvements. (See chapter 12 for a discussion of POM training.)

The MBNQA criteria (chapter 14) is another model for improving the management system. The key concepts of the award examination criteria emphasize the need to evaluate the business' methods, results, and improvement in the seven MBNQA categories. The examination criteria are said to be nonprescriptive; however, the seven categories do generally provide a framework for improvement of the management system.

Solectron Corporation, a 1991 MBNQA winner, conducts regular surveys on a broad range of process and management results, including customer satisfaction of both internal and external customers. Solectron used the MBNQA criteria, employee and customer surveys, and the MBNQA examination process three years in a row to identify weaknesses in its management system and make continuous improvement.

Zytec, another 1991 winner, also stresses the need for employee and customer surveys. Its organizationwide strategic planning process, total participation, and process results are monitored continuously by employees who are empowered to make decisions. The overall cultural transformation of the company is monitored (among other ways) by annual employee surveys (see Bemowski 1991).

As illustrated by Hewlett-Packard, Solectron, and Zytec, the information from employee (internal customers of the management system) and customer surveys should be analyzed and put into a Pareto form, and priorities should be established for future improvement. This process should be repeated regularly as weaknesses in the management system are identified and better processes are put in place. Over time, the quality of the management system and the competitive position of the business are improved.

Management is the process by which businesses bring together resources (people, material, information, and equipment) and orchestrate them to create products and services that have recognized value to the customers. Like every process, management is adaptable to the principles of improvement offered by TQC. The people who do the management process are called managers. They must be willing to learn and improve the process of management in the same manner that they are asking their employees to improve their processes.

SUMMARY

The process of management represents a very sophisticated approach to analyzing weaknesses in the management system and the individual. Successful implementation requires a level of maturity in management that may not exist in all companies and, therefore, this method may not be suitable for all companies at the outset. POM requires that managers be self-confident and mature enough to accept, in a positive manner, the feedback provided by the surveys. Some supervisors and managers may be devastated the first time they see this information. They will need a strong support system and plenty of additional training to help them improve their skills. They must feel secure in their jobs, or the feedback can destabilize their confidence and lead to even poorer performance. In addition, higher managers must not use this information as part of the supervisor's evaluation/rating or backlash will occur. Because of this potential problem, it is best if only the subject of the survey sees the survey feedback. Top management must consider these factors and provide for them before deciding to implement a POM-type system.

SELF-MANAGED TEAMS

Self-managed teams (SMTs) are a relatively new American innovation, which grew out of the concept of quality circles, aimed at achieving higher levels of teamwork and employee involvement. Some examples of successful SMTs can be found at Nummi, Ford Motor Company, Hewlett-Packard, and A. O. Smith.

The aim of SMTs is to increase employee involvement in the decisions of the company to the greatest extent employees' knowledge and training will allow. When this is done successfully, employees enjoy their work more and produce better quality at lower cost. Additionally, the business finds that fewer levels and numbers of managers are required, and the overall responsiveness of the business improves by a considerable amount. The improvement cycle for SMTs is shown in Figure 5.1.

BENEFITS OF SMTs

Quality is directly influenced by SMTs because employees working closest to the process are usually the most knowledgeable about the process and potential quality problems. Employees working as a team to analyze problems and empowered to make changes in the process will do so much more effectively than the bureaucracy of a hierarchical organization.

Productivity is improved because of the better quality achieved and the lowering of scrap and rework. Productivity is also improved when employees enjoy their work, which leads to lower turnover and absenteeism. A reduction in the number of managers also results in improved productivity.

World-class manufacturing technologies

Self-managed teams	Issues and actions	Tools	Training
Improve quality, cost, flexibility			All employees
Form the team *(Understand)*	–How are processes different? –Who works on same process?	–Process flowcharts –Organization charts	–TQC tools –TQM model –Hoshin
Understand the situation	–Do they share common product? –What are team's values? –What are team's measures?	–Corporate values –Personal values –Process quality measures	–Working in groups –Interaction –Word processing
Select an issue *(Select an issue)*	–What authority does team have? –What is team accountable for? To whom? –How is team rewarded?	–Delegation of authority –Quality, cost, delivery –Merit, gain sharing	–Time management –Process of management (POM) –Spreadsheet (Lotus 1-2-3, Excel)
Analyze the process *(Analyze)*	–Are teams empowered to make decisions? –Do teams have needed information to identify issues? –Do teams have time away from daily work to analyze process?	–Pay for knowledge –Access to information systems –Communication –Team time	–Peer evaluation –Kepner–Tregoe problem analysis
Plan a change *(Plan)*	–Do teams understand bigger process to plan change and understand potential problems? –Can they analyze benefits? –Does team have resources? –Has bureaucracy been eliminated?	–Design of experiments –Potential problem analysis –Return on investment	
Implement the plan *(Do)*		–Training dollars –Flatter organizations –Less vertical approval	
Verify the results *(Check)*	–Teams review own results. –Communicate results to customers and interested parties.	–TQC tools –Information systems	
Make routine *(Act)*	–Changes are documented and made part of process. –Celebrate results. –Move to next opportunity.	–Production change orders –Poka yoke –Have a lunch, cake, etc. –Kaizen	

Continuous improvement (kaizen)

Figure 5.1. SMTs and the improvement cycle.

As quality and productivity improve, flexibility and responsiveness will also improve. Responsiveness is generally limited by the ability of the employees in a process to make quick changes in setups and to change over to different parts or products. The absence of quality problems and bureaucracy enables teams to make decisions very quickly and implement needed changes without undue delays.

THE STRUCTURE OF THE SMT

A team is a group of people who work within a common process or with a common task and set of objectives. While there is no prescribed size, most run in numbers between five and 10 people. Once the teams are trained and functional, one manager or supervisor can facilitate the activities of several teams.

In an SMT environment, the division of responsibilities for managers and employees is different than in the traditional hierarchical structure. Management's primary responsibility here is to empower the team. This is done by giving the team authority to act, removing obstacles, and establishing a suitable reward system. Specifically, management is responsible for providing

- Clear and reasonable objectives
- The proper tools and equipment
- Training
- Empowerment—authority to act
- A fair reward system
- Feedback and evaluation

Given these items, the team is accountable for the results of

- Quality
- Cost
- Delivery
- Service levels
- Peer feedback
- Continuous improvement
- Planning
- Decision making

This division of responsibility empowers the team to act when necessary and with a minimum amount of bureaucracy. The primary concern of the manager is whether the team's decisions and actions are consistent with the agreed-upon objectives. Does this mean that the team makes all the decisions? No, it means that once the team has demonstrated the ability to make decisions, it is allowed to do so. As the team becomes better trained and more capable, it will make increasingly more important decisions. Businesses that have been successful in implementing SMTs have reduced the number of managers by a factor of 2–4 times below traditional levels.

PROFIT SHARING AND KNOWLEDGE-BASED PAY

There are two reward factors that most people associate with successful team implementation. The first is some form of profit-sharing or gain-sharing compensation. The second is a knowledge pay system.

Gain sharing has a broader definition than profit sharing, and can relate directly to profits or be based on improvements in quality and/or reductions in cost (that is, productivity improvements). Most advocates of gain-sharing programs recommend that the income derived from gain sharing be approximately 25 percent of total income. If the amount is too small, it fails to provide the motivation; if it is too large, the risk for employees becomes too great. Gain sharing should be done equally for members of a team or department, based on group results.

Knowledge-based pay is that part of the pay which is variable, based on individual knowledge and skill. Dr. Edward Lawler of the University of Southern California (Lawler 1987) uses a three-dimensional cube to describe the factors that should govern knowledge-based pay (see Figure 5.2). The horizontal skills represent the variety of tasks the individual is capable of performing. The vertical skills represent the management tasks learned and practiced by the person. The depth of skill is the quality and productivity of the person's skills.

These factors help provide the correct incentives for the desired behavior and must be structured differently for each environment. For example, a high-variety, flexible manufacturing environment places a higher value on the individual's ability to do a variety of tasks. In a totally cooperative team environment, employees must do most of the tasks traditionally assigned to managers. They must therefore be skilled in management tasks. And lastly, the quality and productivity skills for these tasks are the areas traditionally evaluated in a merit-pay system. They must also be included.

In businesses where these methods have been successful, first-level employees have always been involved in designing these systems. First-level employees usually understand the needs of the process best. They are also, of course, the ones who best understand their own motivations and needs. By tapping this knowledge at the outset, employers reduce the risk of employee backlash when implementing this kind of change to the pay system.

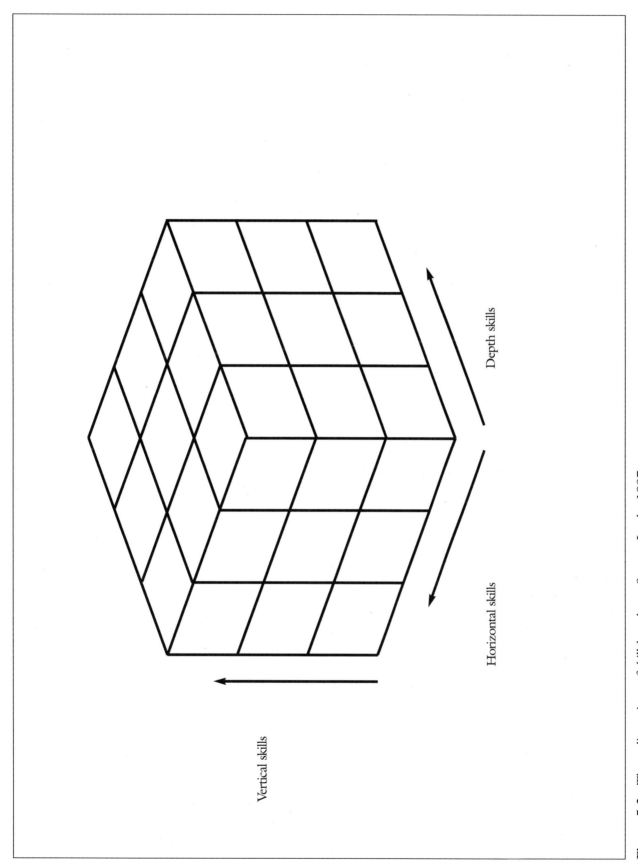

Figure 5.2. Three dimensions of skill-based pay. Source: Lawler 1987.

25

SUMMARY

Self-managed teams are sometimes referred to as self-directed work teams. The choice of titles implies that in the minds of some, employees are capable of directing their own activities but not of managing themselves. This may also say something about the scope of the activities about which employees are allowed to make decisions. The concept of self-management is aimed at reducing the hierarchical management structure. The teams must be capable of all decisions—peer evaluation, planning, and work direction—before this can happen. If this is done properly, the company will enjoy the benefits of improved quality, higher productivity, and increased flexibility and responsiveness.

QUALITY FUNCTION DEPLOYMENT

To be successful in a highly competitive market, businesses must be more precise in understanding customer needs and in designing and manufacturing products that meet those needs. Much of the Japanese economic success is attributable to their ability to do this better than their U.S. counterparts. Part of the reason is that they use a very structured and analytical approach to defining customer needs in terms that lead to better quality products and processes. This approach is commonly referred to as quality function deployment. (See Figure 6.1 for the QFD improvement cycle.)

QFD was pioneered by Toyota Auto Body in 1975 (Sullivan 1990). Since then, it has been improved and expanded for use in most Japanese companies. Many U.S. companies have also begun to use QFD with a fair degree of success. Some notable examples include Ford Motor Company, General Motors, and International Telephone and Telegraph. At this time, the American Supplier Institute (ASI) estimates that there are literally thousands of QFD applications in progress in the United States.

The aim of QFD is to create cross-functional interaction and cooperation toward applying the *voice of the customer* to products and processes. The Japanese concept of QFD entails harvesting the knowledge of production workers, engineers, and managers in a collective decision-making process that leads to continuous improvement of customer satisfaction. Consistent with traditional Japanese thinking, they emphasize the value of using the knowledge of the group over the genius of a few technocrats.

World-class manufacturing technologies

Quality function deployment	Issues and actions	Tools	Training
Improve quality, cost, flexibility			
Form the team *(Understand)*	–Cross-functional team –Marketing, design, production	–SMTs –QCs –Project teams	All employees –Working in groups –TQC tools –SMT tools –Benchmarking –Hoshin –Taguchi quality loss function
Understand the situation	–Who are the customers? –What products are needed? –What are customers' requirements? –How well do we meet requirements?	–New seven tools –Benchmarking	
Select an issue *(Select an issue)*	–Which requirements are most important? –Which requirements will we meet? –What product will be offered?	–House of quality –100 dollar test	
Analyze the process *(Analyze)*	–What product specifications are required? –What technologies will be used?	–House of quality –Product plan	
Plan a change *(Plan)*	–What are process requirements? –What are part requirements? –What are production requirements?	–Process plan –Material deployment plan –Production plan	Engineers –DFM, DFA, DFQ, DFX –Taguchi design of experiments –House of quality –Weibull analysis –Reliability growth –Accelerated experiments
Implement the plan *(Do)*	–Make investments. –Design products and processes. –Design experiments. –Design and process simulation.	–Investment decision analysis –DFM, DFA, DFQ, DFX –Design of experiments –CAD/CAE/CIM	
Verify the results *(Check)*	–Do stress testing. –Monitor production status.	–Reliability analysis –Seven tools –Quality loss function analysis	
Make routine *(Act)*	–Document designs. –Document procedures. –Make tooling. –Move to next opportunity.	–Poka yoke –Kaizen	
Continuous improvement (kaizen)			

Figure 6.1. QFD and the improvement cycle.

FOUR PHASES OF QFD

Phase I: Product Planning

The most popular phase used by U.S. businesses, phase I is the product planning phase used to translate customer wants into product parameters. Phase I is facilitated by a house of quality, which is a matrix showing customer wants on one axis and product specifications on the other axis. The customer wants are described in terms relevant to the customer's application (for example, "paint that hides well"). The product parameters are described in terms of the technology needed to provide the customer need (for example, viscosity and titanium content). The house over the matrix is used to show correlation between the product specifications.

Phase II: Product Planning

Phase II relates primarily to product engineering functions. In this phase, design parameters are transferred to part characteristics and the creation of target values, which represent the best values for fit, function, and appearance. The ASI estimates that approximately half of the U.S. companies using QFD have progressed through phase II.

Phase III: Process Planning

Most of the activities associated with phases I and II are performed by product engineering functions. In phases III and IV it is essential to involve production engineers, supervisors, and production operators. Phase III is where product engineering parameters are transferred to process parameters for production and assembly. In this phase, production capabilities for each activity are established and target values are set for continuous improvement. Very few U.S. companies have utilized this phase.

Phase IV: Production Planning

In the last stage of QFD the target values from the process planning phase are transferred to production standards. This phase makes the final link complete—from the voice of the customer, through engineering, to the daily activities of the production worker. Following through the thought process behind the four phases, one can see a continuous refinement of customer needs that involves many people from throughout the factory.

KEY ELEMENTS OF QFD

QFD is a very structured process of customer needs deployment, which is very dependent on employee involvement and knowledge, and requires employee training in the establishment and improvement of process and production target values.

Japanese companies report that the greatest benefit in quality and cost savings comes from phases III and IV, which is where U.S. companies have made the least progress. The latter phases require a different training emphasis to be successful, and most U.S. companies have not yet addressed this issue.

The traditional approach to training is to provide all technical improvement courses to engineers and managers in order to make them the experts. This might include all of the statistical training for understanding variability, QFD, and Taguchi loss functions. Production operators, on the other hand, are provided with training in machine operation, blueprint reading, and the use of measurement tools. This separate-but-equal approach to training inhibits the involvement of production operators in improving the quality and cost of their processes.

The Japanese approach is to provide more overlap in the training for engineers and production workers. This is especially true in areas of SPC and quality loss functions. Employees are evaluated based on their use of these tools as well as on their general process skills. One example involves the use of the Taguchi quality loss function, which can be applied by anybody with an eighth-grade math education and a handheld calculator. The Taguchi loss function simply enables operators to see the losses in a process due to variability and to calculate cost savings associated with reducing variability. This tool is an important part of the QFD phases III and IV.

SUMMARY

QFD is a highly structured method for applying the voice of the customer to products and processes. This is done by using a matrix called a *house of quality* to define the product's external and internal specifications.

QFD is still in its infancy in its application by U.S. business. The automobile industry is by far the predominant user of QFD; however, great strides are being made in other industries, particularly the software industry. QFD finds particular importance in companies that are making the transition from being technology driven to market driven. The difference is that technology-driven companies defined their products by the next new technology and speculated, based on the engineering intuition, about what would be important to the customer. Market-driven companies look at customer needs first, and then find technologies that will best enable them to meet those needs.

As with other WCM tools, success with QFD requires highly integrated teamwork. Engineering, sales, production, and quality assurance teams must all participate in the QFD process. These teams must be trained to work together, as well as in the methods of analyzing customer needs.

DESIGN FOR MANUFACTURING

Design for manufacturing (DFM) can be viewed as a subset of QFD in the management system. QFD focuses on creating a customer voice in the design and manufacture of the product; DFM is specifically aimed at improving quality and reducing cost within the context of fulfilling customer needs (see Figure 7.1). In this respect, DFM fulfills phases II, III, and IV of the QFD model.

The principles of DFM are derived from a cost-driver concept. Cost drivers are the individual factors and decisions that are made about the design of the product and process that influence or *drive* manufacturing costs. Process factors include such things as process defect rates, choice of material delivery systems (JIT or batch), levels of automation, and so on. Process costs depend on the choices managers make. The product design factors include such things as the number of parts, number of process steps, variability of the parts, and robustness of design (a term that defines how consistently the product goes together and stays together without problems under varying conditions) (Taguchi 1980). An engineer's design decisions influence how much the product will cost based on some additional management decisions about choices of processes. The process of designing for manufacturability results in design decisions that drive the lowest amount of manufacturing cost and utilize the lowest cost processes. Some examples of how DFM influences cost are shown in Table 7.1.

As Table 7.1 shows, quality—in terms of part variability, part reliability, and design stresses—is a key factor in a design for manufacturing strategy. Design decisions about the parts also affect the processes required. For example, certain part designs can only be

World-class manufacturing technologies

Design for manufacture	Issues and actions	Tools	Training
Improve quality, cost, flexibility			
Form the team (*Understand*)	–Design, production, suppliers –Concurrent engineering teams	–QCs, SMTs –Project team	All employees –Working in groups –TQC tools –SMT tools –Benchmarking –Hoshin –Taguchi quality loss functions –Boothroid analysis –Process costing systems
Understand the situation	–What are customer needs? –What are product cost goals? –What are product quality goals? –What are part specifications?	–House of quality –Component data base –Manufacturing process data base	
Select an issue (*Select an issue*)	–Which parts and processes have the most variability? –Which parts drive the most cost? –Identify critical parts.	–Design of experiments –Process cost systems –Boothroid analysis	
Analyze the process (*Analyze*)	–What features of the part or process drive the cost so high? –Can the part or process be simplified?	–Process cost drivers	Engineers –Taguchi design of experiments –House of quality –Weibull analysis –Reliability growth –Accelerated experiments
Plan a change (*Plan*)	–Redesign the part or process. –Select new parts. –Select new process.	–Design tools	
Implement the plan (*Do*)	–Simulate process. –Make parts.	–Design of experiments –CAD/CAE/CIM tools –Prototype shop	
Verify the results (*Check*)	–Check quality and cost.	–Seven tools –Reliability analysis	
Make routine (*Act*)	–Document results. –Make fixtures/tooling. –Move to next opportunity.	–Quality loss function analysis –Poka yoke –Kaizen	
Continuous improvement (kaizen)			

Figure 7.1. DFM and the improvement cycle.

Table 7.1. DFM decisions versus cost and quality results.

Design decision	Result
Large number of part numbers	More stock locations More suppliers More buyers Higher cost
More part variability	More scrap More rework More tests More technicians More production engineers Higher cost Lower quality
More process steps	More setups More handling More defects More rework Higher cost Lower quality
More part failures	More scrap More problems to solve More rework More service cost More tests More engineers Higher cost Lower quality

machined by certain pieces of equipment. As some types of equipment produce better quality than others, a de facto decision is made in the design stage about the quality of the part. Ultimately, the quality of the product, as seen by the customer, is equally influenced by these decisions. This sounds very much like phases II, III, and IV of QFD, which is why some people treat DFM as a subset of QFD.

Productivity is also influenced by design decisions. Product design quality influences cost directly through scrap and rework. Additionally, there are factors like number of parts, part numbers, and process steps. These factors are often associated with variety and are sometimes unavoidable in a high-variety environment. The DFM charter should be to use as many common parts as possible in the designs. Care should be taken to maximize the volume on individual part numbers and use common processes and suppliers to the greatest extent possible.

Flexibility is a major beneficiary of the DFM strategy. As noted, productivity is influenced by part numbers, process steps, and suppliers. Fewer parts and suppliers enable the business to more easily function in a JIT environment, which has its own cost-saving features. Also, use of more common parts and processes means that the business has more flexibility in its daily production schedules. One of the biggest inhibitors to flexibility is product-specific inventory and machinery.

The people most able to influence DFM strategies are the engineers. However, as in the use of QFD, production floor supervisors and workers must also be involved. Much of the knowledge about the costs and quality of individual processes resides in the minds of the production workers. They must be included in design decisions to ensure that the necessary information about process performance is factored into the design decision.

SUMMARY

While DFM can be thought of as a subset of QFD, it does have its own place in a WCM strategy. DFM focuses on the product and process capability. DFM presumes that the proverbial wall between engineering and manufacturing is real and must be eliminated. The wall is eliminated when engineering and manufacturing collaborate on product and process designs, so that the cost drivers of the design are reduced to their lowest levels and customer satisfaction is at its highest level.

A key part of the DFM strategy is, strangely enough, the accounting system. Activity-based accounting (ABC) systems provide visibility into the cost of the processes by activity. Manufacturing can use ABC systems to characterize the process' costs. Manufacturing can collect ABC information and apply it to the designer's process and parts data base, thereby allowing the engineer to receive immediate feedback on the choice of a part or process.

In recent years, companies have started to use a term called DFX, which implies design for whatever you want to designate X to mean. Thus, X could stand for cost, quality, serviceability, or any other business need. In any case, the principles are the same and can be summarized as (1) understand the end result that is desired in the product, (2) identify the key measures of performance, and (3) provide the tools and incentives to achieve the desired results.

AUTOMATION

Economists teach that 80 percent of the productivity improvements over the history of the world have come about through the development and application of technology. Automation (ATM), whether in the form of automated machinery, robotics, computers, or otherwise, is the product of technological development. As certainly as technology is developing more rapidly in today's environment, so are the choices, quality, productivity, and flexibility of new machinery.

The improvements come from the application of a continuous improvement cycle as shown in Figure 8.1. As the quality, cost, and flexibility of the new technologies improve, the return on investment for technology becomes more attractive. In many situations it is possible to predict when it will be more effective to apply a new technology to a given task. This is true regardless of whether the process is completed by a person or a machine. As new technologies are applied, the requirement for unskilled manual labor decreases and the need for technically skilled operators and maintenance workers increases. Lower-skilled employees must continue to learn and develop new skills to become more employable in the highly technical environment.

Many Japanese companies that have invested heavily in automation say they have done so more in the interest of improving quality and flexibility than in reducing cost. They are also frequently quoted as saying that automation is necessary because of a national shortage of labor. Whatever their motives, there is a common theme associated with implementation in a TQM environment—simplify before automating.

World-class manufacturing technologies

Automation	Issues and actions	Tools	Training
Improve quality, cost, flexibility			All employees
Form the team — *Understand*	–Process teams	–QCs, SMTs	–SMTs, QCs
Understand the situation	–What are customer needs? –What is process capability? –What technologies are being used? –Are there new technologies available?	–QFD, TPM, TPL –Process information data base –Process plan/documentation –WCM studies	–Process costing systems –ROI analysis –TQC tools –Blueprint reading –Equipment operation and maintenance
Select an issue — *Select an issue*	–Do new forms of automation provide ROI—cost, quality, flexibility? –Where does the greatest ROI exist? –Pick type of automation	–Specification sheets –ROI analysis –Seven tools	
Analyze the process — *Analyze*	–Flowchart the process. –Is it possible to simplify process? –How does automation fit into the process?	–Flowcharts –New seven tools –Design of experiments –ROI analysis	
Plan a change — *Plan*	–Do ROI analysis. –Redesign process. –What new training is required?	–Design tools –Supplier information	
Implement the plan — *Do*	–Purchase equipment. –Train operators.	–Budget costs	
Verify the results — *Check*	–Monitor production or prototype results.	–Seven tools	
Make routine — *Act*	–Document new procedures. –Make fixtures/tooling. –Move to next opportunity.	–Poka yoke –Kaizen	
Continuous improvement (kaizen)			

Figure 8.1. Automation and the improvement cycle.

There are two primary reasons for simplification before automation. One is that the simpler the task, the easier it is to write computer programs and electronic work instructions to perform the work. Simplification thus lowers the cost of automation and improves the quality. The second is to minimize the number of variables in the material. This is a form of simplification which has benefits similar to the first item.

Automated machinery does an excellent job of repeating a task in exactly the same way, which minimizes the chances of error. However, if the machine is set up incorrectly, it is just as capable of continuously producing errors. Quality is enhanced by this consistency. Generally speaking, machines also have much greater control for doing very precise work. There are many types of work that are so precise that the work could not be done without machinery. This is becoming more true every day.

Productivity is enhanced by ATM because machinery is generally capable of completing repetitive tasks much faster than humans and with a lower probability of error. This becomes more true over time, as wages increase and the cost of technology decreases.

ATM can be very effective at improving flexibility if setup times are minimized. Most forms of modern automation are electronically controlled, which allows work instructions to be stored in electronic data bases. The rapid availability of the instructions make it possible to change from one part to another quickly, with a minimum of setup time and errors.

TYPES OF AUTOMATION

Every industry has a unique set of automation requirements and therefore, it is impossible to cover all the possibilities here. Figure 8.2 illustrates some of the different types of automation in use for different aspects of the process. Some of these technologies, however, are finding widespread use in all industries and, therefore are described here.

Bar code. All parts and products are marked with a bar code which can be read by an optical scanner. The bar code contains all relevant information about the part. The bar code technology replaces the need for people to type information into the computer, thereby reducing the chances for error. Bar codes are also much faster, as evidenced in the supermarket checkout line where they are now widely used. Manufacturers use barcodes to receive parts from suppliers, to track material through the process, to pull material from storerooms, and to verify and ship products and accessories.

Computerized instructions. A few businesses have removed all paper assembly instructions from the production floor. They have replaced them with a computer screen that allows assemblers access to all relevant assembly instructions, which are stored in a computer

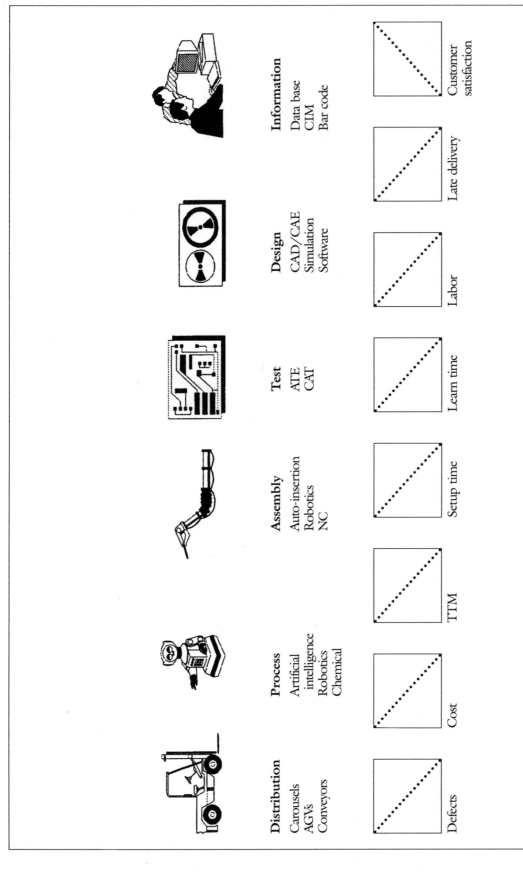

Figure 8.2. Process applications for automation.

data base. The operator has up-to-date drawings and/or video images from which to work. The paperless documentation has proven to improve quality, increase productivity, shorten learning curves, shorten setup times, and increase employee flexibility in the process.

Computerized data collection. Quality reporting has been automated in many factories. Sometimes it is integrated with the paperless documentation, when it exists; other times, it is a stand-alone system. In either event, quality information collected in this manner is readily available for analysis by quality circles and self-managed teams. The availability of this information in graphical form speeds the process of quality improvement and cuts down the team's analysis time, thus achieving greater productivity. There are two types of data that can be collected. One type is called *parametric test data*. This type of data can be collected directly from a piece of electronic test equipment without human involvement. The other type of data relates to part failures and replacement. The latter information is usually recorded via a computer terminal at the time a defective part is replaced.

Electronic mail. Communications are an important part of every organization, and affect quality, productivity, and flexibility. Electronic mail and voice mail are two technological innovations that greatly enhance communication by making messages immediately available 24 hours a day just about anywhere in the world.

Electronic data interchange (EDI). EDI is a modern technology that enables manufacturers to communicate design information electronically between remote sites. Some manufacturers send drawings and schematics directly to suppliers whose machines are set up electronically to produce the parts on demand. EDI allows design centers to almost instantaneously communicate, via satellite, their designs to several remote manufacturing sites anywhere in the world.

SUMMARY

Historical gains in productivity can be closely linked to advances in the development and application of technology. Even so, automation does not guarantee success. Automation for the sake of automation can just as easily lead to technological gridlock. As in all cases of applying WCM technology, management judgment is required in determining how much automation is enough.

There are many factors to be considered in ATM, including the cost of labor versus technology; the product, in terms of how well it lends itself to automation (that is, variety and variability); and the product volume requirements. As one looks around the world, it is apparent that automation may be a necessity in high-priced labor markets like Japan. However, even Japanese companies do not automate many manufacturing companies in the People's Republic of China, because labor rates are so low.

Well-conceived automation strategies can lead to improvements in quality, cost, and flexibility. However management must consider each of the factors discussed in this chapter. If management uses good judgment in these areas, it will probably find that some combination of automation and human resources will be needed.

COMPUTER-INTEGRATED MANUFACTURING

Automation and computer-integrated manufacturing (CIM) work hand-in-hand to continuously improve the business. CIM is the result of technological development and investment in information technology which must be continuously nurtured and improved upon as shown in Figure 9.1. The cyclical improvement over time ensures that opportunities are continuously evaluated and acted upon to take the best advantage of new technologies.

CIM is the foundation for information exchange in the fully integrated factory. Sometimes CIM is described to mean *complete information management*. The function of CIM is to use computers, networks, and cables to link together all the information needs of the people and processes in the factory. One manager described CIM as being JIT information, using the analogy of JIT material. CIM enables workers and machines to have information available in the right amounts, with the right quality, and just in time for use.

There are many different types of information necessary in a factory. Design information must be passed from design to production; information about materials, costs, inventory, and suppliers must be available for purchasing and accounting; managers and workers need information about quality, schedules, and orders; and programmed instructions are needed for automated machinery. During the last 20 years, computers have gained an increasing role in managing this information.

The ever-increasing use of automation and computers in manufacturing presented a challenge to information technologists.

World-class manufacturing technologies

Computer-integrated manufacturing	Issues and actions	Tools	Training
Improve quality, cost, flexibility	—CIM team—information technology (IT), production, design	—SMTs, project teams	
Form the team (*Understand*)	—What are equipment information needs? —What management information is needed?	—Data sheets —Surveys —Organization charts —Process flow diagrams —Process requirements —Individual requirements	All employees —Working in groups —Surveys —Flowcharting —TQC tools —Process/equipment operator knowledge
Understand the situation	—What is needed by engineers? —What is needed by production workers? —Where is information needed? —What is source of information?		
Select an issue (*Select an issue*)	—Flowchart process and information flows. —Can process be simplified?	—Flowcharts —New seven tools	
Analyze the process (*Analyze*)	—Who supplies the information? —Can information be electronically linked?	—Process flow diagrams —Users' needs analysis	Information technology engineers —Data base structures —Programming —System interface capabilities —EDI —Specific equipment knowledge
Plan a change (*Plan*)	—Design a CIM architecture. —Assign responsibilities and budgets.	—Drafting tools —Hoshin	
Implement the plan (*Do*)	—Put equipment in place. —Run parallel experiment with existing process.		
Verify the results (*Check*)	—Compare results.	—Seven tools	
Make routine (*Act*)	—Turn off manual system. —Document process. —Move to next opportunity.	—Poka yoke —Kaizen	

Continuous improvement (kaizen)

Figure 9.1. CIM and the improvement cycle.

Many of the systems were designed with special and different information needs. There was not an easy way to link them together, creating what some people have referred to as *islands of automation*. In this environment, a considerable amount of double handling is required to move information between systems, which adds to the probability of errors. Double handling is also very time consuming.

CIM ties all of these systems together by creating common data bases and neutral data formats. (see Figure 9.2). The goal of the CIM system is to facilitate the electronic interchange of information. This goal is easily achieved where automated machinery is the end user of the information. Machines and/or robots can directly access programming instruction from an electronic data base. Engineers can access process and material information directly from a data base and make the best cost and quality decisions on new designs. Engineers can also send design information directly to machinery to get prototype parts made with very fast turnaround. The possibilities for CIM are almost endless, and present an ongoing challenge to information technologists.

CIM has had a dramatic effect on improving quality. Today's information technology is extremely accurate. Process errors have been reduced by over 100 times just by improving the accuracy of the data transfer. Additionally, CIM contributes to better-quality designs by enabling engineers to simulate manufacture before releasing designs to production. Computers also make it easy to ensure that the best-quality parts and processes are selected.

Productivity is also dramatically impacted by CIM. Today's computers are fast, and information to manufacture a part can be passed to a machine in fractions of a second. Computers, therefore, reduce the amount of time and energy required to handle and process information. CIM and automation together reduce the time required for material handling, assembly, management, and administration. It can impact just about every aspect of the factory floor.

CIM also impacts flexibility. In high-variety manufacturing environments, many different setups per day are required at a single workstation. CIM enables setup instructions and process information to be immediately available to the machine or operators. This allows for quick changeovers, which in turn aids responsiveness and the ability to produce high variety at low volumes, and with good quality and low cost.

SUMMARY

CIM functions to eliminate islands of automation through JIT information flow. CIM provides the framework to ensure that accurate information is available where needed and at the right time

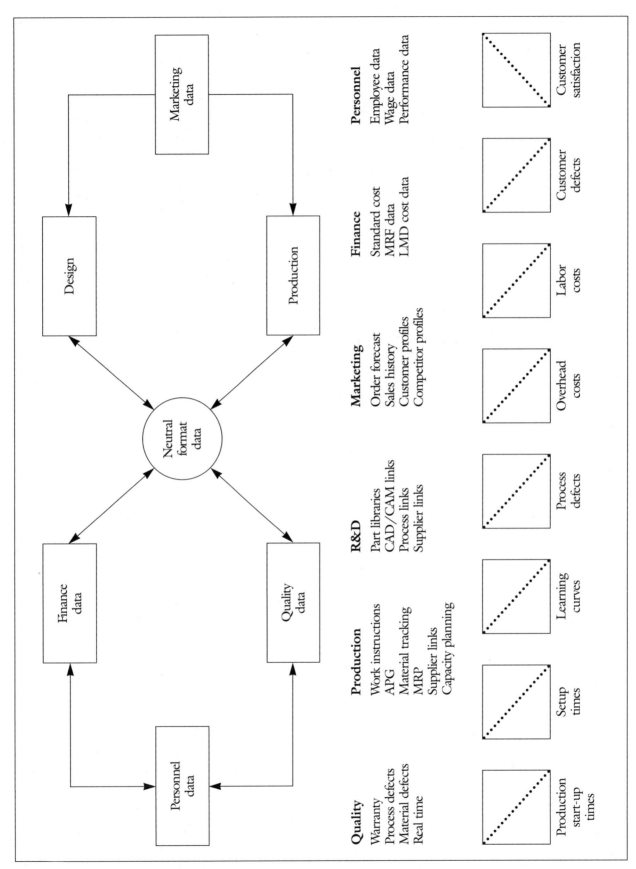

Figure 9.2. The simple CIM block diagram.

to help achieve the task required of a person or process. The CIM system can lead to better quality, cost, and flexibility, through better utilization of automation, DFM systems, communications, and other management systems. The absence of a coherent CIM strategy will result in poor performance of every major system in which accurate and timely information is required.

JUST-IN-TIME PRODUCTION

Just-in-time (JIT) is a material management philosophy that enables a business to improve quality, reduce inventory and space, and improve responsiveness to customers by reducing cycle and delivery times. The name JIT implies that all material is pulled forward to the point of use in just the right amounts and at just the right time, thereby eliminating unnecessary inventory queues and costs. The improvement cycle for JIT is shown in Figure 10.1.

JIT methods were perfected in the Japanese automobile industry, most notably by Toyota. There are primarily two types of JIT systems used: the continuous-flow system and the kanban system. The continuous-flow system is usually used on a high-volume, single-product line. In this system, the line is loaded with the right amount of inventory and the work is passed from one station to another at a pace predetermined by the slowest process in the line.

Kanban, on the other hand, requires that work not start at a process until a kanban signal (card) is received from a downstream process, signaling that it needs another part. The kanban system is most frequently used in manufacturing environments that are highly flexible and where considerable amount of variety is produced.

Quality is impacted both directly and indirectly. It is impacted directly, because JIT requires less inventory which sits idle for shorter periods of time. The inventory is therefore less subject to the hazards of the environment and the possibility of physical damage. Also, the low amounts of inventory enable engineering changes to be implemented with lesser amounts of rework, which tends to be a defect-prone process. The indirect quality benefits of

World-class manufacturing technologies

Just-in-time	Issues and actions	Tools	Training
Improve quality, cost, flexibility			
Form the team *(Understand)*	–Production control team –What material is needed where? –What are process queues? –Where are bottlenecks? –What volume/variety is needed? –What is actual process time? –What delivery time is needed? –Where is most inventory?	–SMTs, project teams –A process flowchart –A bill of materials –Work-in-process inventory accounts –Work order tracking system –Material requirements planning (MRP)	All employees –Working in groups –Flowcharting –Kanban functions –JIT theory –TPC tools
Understand the situation *(Select an issue)*	–Where will JIT provide greatest benefit? –Where is least risk? –Pick process/parts.	–New seven tools –Design of experiments –ROI analysis	Production control –MPS –ABOM –MRP –MAP –Design of experiments –JIT simulation tools –Post deduct–back flush accounting
Select an issue			
Analyze the process *(Analyze)*	–Where is material needed? –What are daily volumes? –Who will resupply? –How long does resupply take?	–Master production plan –MRP –Cycle time measurements	
Plan a change *(Plan)*	–Design the flows. –Specify queues and kanban inventory. –Design resupply signals. –Specify cycle times. –Do an experiment, if possible.	–Flowcharts –Kanban –JIT simulation tools	
Implement the plan *(Do)*	–Train operators. –Train suppliers. –Start process.	–Kanban training	
Verify the results *(Check)*	–Monitor results of cycle time, throughput and queues, quality, inventory, and delivery time.	–Seven tools	
Make routine *(Act)*	–Document process. –Move to next opportunity.	–Poka yoke –Kaizen	
Continuous improvement (kaizen)			

Figure 10.1. JIT and the improvement cycle.

JIT are achieved because in a JIT environment, inventory arrives where needed, just in time to be used. Quality problems require the production line to stop (the Japanese use the term *jidohka*) until they are fixed. If there are many quality problems, the line has to be shut down continuously, with zero output instead of zero inventories. Thus, the JIT system requires that quality problems not be passed on, and that a highly effective TQC improvement process be used to eliminate problems once they are discovered.

There are many productivity benefits associated with JIT. They include improved quality, less scrap and rework, less paperwork, fewer work orders and tracking documents, less inventory, less capital investment, less space, fewer inventory storage bins, less material handling cost, and less double handling of parts.

JIT also makes a big contribution to flexibility. Flexibility is measured by the ability of the business to respond to changing customer requirements and provide short delivery times. A primary factor in achieving higher levels of flexibility is cycle time. Cycle time is the time it takes to run a part through the process from start to finish. JIT shortens cycle time by eliminating inventory queues.

ELEMENTS OF JIT

Three aspects of JIT are needed to achieve full implementation. Figure 10.2 will aid in visualizing these functions.

1. Build-to-order (BTO)—Customer JIT

2. Production JIT

3. Supplier JIT

Build to order. BTO, or customer JIT, establishes the delivery time between the customer and the business. In the past, long cycle times in the factory made it necessary for businesses to either carry a large amount of finished goods inventory to meet a variety of customer needs, or to have long delivery times, in which case the customer had to wait weeks or months to receive an order. Short cycle time and flexible manufacturing enable the business to offer both short delivery times and keep finished goods inventory to a minimum.

Production JIT. Production JIT is set up on a line with successive processes adjusted to take about the same amount of time. Sometimes the line is set up in a *U* shape so that the product starts and finishes at about the same location. Material is stored at each process in small quantities as required to do a fixed amount of work, which may range from minutes to days of work. As the part is passed along the line, material and labor are added at each successive step. This is very much like a salad bar. In a continuous-flow process the inventory usages are timed so that new inventory

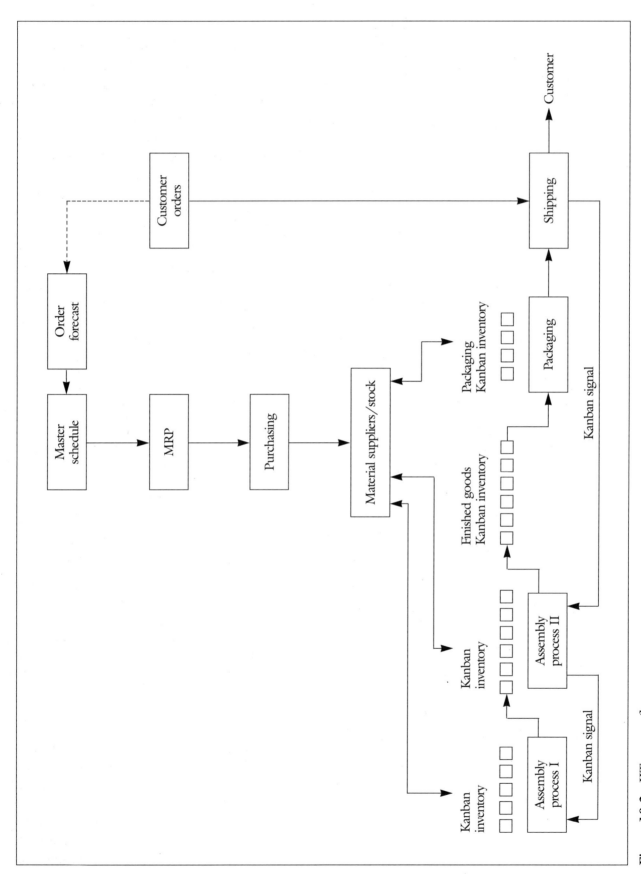

Figure 10.2. JIT process flow.

is always arriving before the inventory is depleted. In a kanban process, a card is sent to the supplier or storeroom to retrieve more parts when the kanban queue reaches a critical level.

Supplier JIT. It is possible to operate with a BTO and production JIT system without supplier JIT; in fact, many companies do this. The downside to this, however, is that a considerable amount of inventory is still kept in the storeroom at great cost. It also requires that parts be handled twice—once putting them into stock and once taking them out to distribute.

JIT supplier delivery circumvents this problem by having suppliers be part of the delivery chain or kanban system. The parts are received from suppliers and delivered directly to the point on the production line where they are to be used. Often, the variety of parts and suppliers is so large that this is difficult to achieve. In these cases, manufacturers will usually focus on parts that are high cost, high volume, and/or costly to handle and store. By focusing on these parts in a Pareto fashion, steady improvement is made toward higher levels of supplier JIT.

Suppliers can work in the kanban chain by using electronic kanban signals or facsimile machines to signal stock requirements. Initially, suppliers may find it necessary to store needed parts in their finished goods inventory (FGI) until they learn how to shorten their cycle times. Even this method, though not ideal, may still be more cost effective for the manufacturer than storing that same inventory in its stockroom and double handling the material.

SUMMARY

The Japanese automobile industry pushed JIT concepts to the limit in the 1980s, and many U.S. companies followed. JIT strategies enabled them to produce a variety of cars with very short lead times. Recently, however, some Japanese companies, like Toyota, have begun to change their JIT strategy. They have begun to cut back on the number of models offered, and reduce the frequency of material deliveries—all in an effort to cut costs (Goozner 1993).

Does this spell an end to the usefulness of JIT strategies in WCM? Not at all; it simply means that Japanese companies are adjusting their strategies to the changing environment. The Japanese and others have long recognized that there is a trade-off between variety and cost. WCM methods such as JIT and ATM help mitigate the cost with higher variety, but they do not completely compensate. Recently, the value of the yen relative to the dollar has put increasing pressure on Japanese exports and, thus, forced them to move further down the cost/variety curve. The change in Japanese strategy is a simple reminder that the cost/variety balance is sometimes precarious, and changing economies may cause companies to shift one way or the other.

THE MANAGEMENT SYSTEM

The elements of TQM and world-class manufacturing discussed thus far have been presented individually and, to some extent, as shown in Tables 1.1, 1.2, and 1.3, in relation to one another. These WCM methods and TQM also can be viewed in the context of a management system. To help create a view of the TQM management system, let's first review the Japanese approach to TQM.

Traditional Japanese TQM models focus management attention on five areas. These five categories of Japanese TQM are listed below and defined in subsequent paragraphs.

1. Management commitment
2. Leadership
3. Customer focus
4. Total participation
5. Process analysis and improvement

CATEGORY 1: MANAGEMENT COMMITMENT

People and capital investment are included in this category because they represent commitments that management must make to create a business with the culture, knowledge, and equipment needed to serve the market it has chosen to address. Management commitment must be enhanced through the process of continuous improvement shown in Figure 11.1.

Employees. People's attitudes must be continuously improved to trust and be supportive of the goals of the business. People must be viewed as important assets and be provided the training

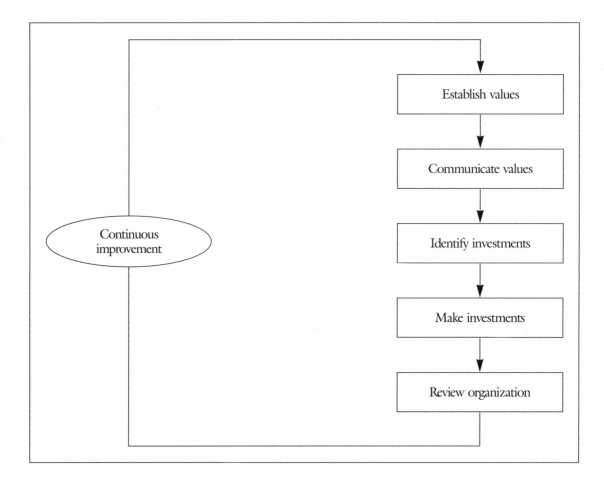

Figure 11.1. Management commitment and continuous improvement.

necessary to be effective in the type of technological environment required of the business. Management must commit to and practice a set of values that continuously reinforce these principles.

Capital investment. Each business has a different purpose, mission, and technology. These differences require different types and levels of processes and capitalization to effectively shape the business to its environment. Management must commit the correct level of capitalization and continuously seek to improve it.

CATEGORY 2: LEADERSHIP

Planning and motivation are in the category of leadership because they represent management's responsibility to provide direction and encouragement to the business. This category is analogous to the helm of a ship, where decisions and control are exercised to move the ship in one direction or another and at different speeds. Leadership is continuously improved through the process shown in Figure 11.2.

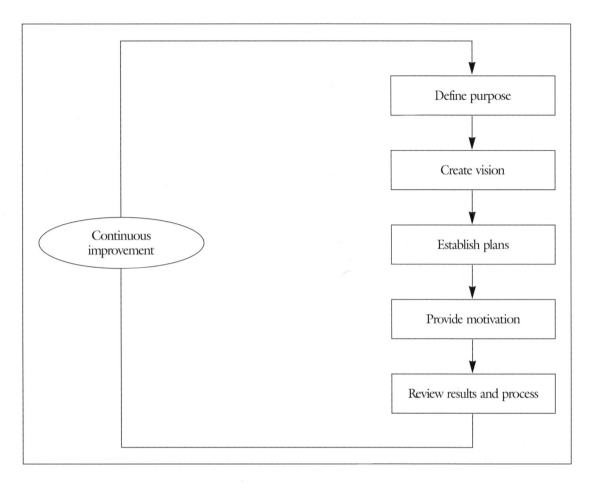

Figure 11.2. Leadership and continuous improvement.

Plans. The business and its employees are guided by a set of plans. The plans state the purpose, visions, goals, and strategies for the organization. The planning system can be efficient or inefficient. If the planning system is inefficient, employees will spend too much time working on the plans and, worse, spend too much time working on the wrong things. Management must continuously examine the effectiveness of the planning system and seek to improve it.

Motivation. The rate of a business' progress in its chosen direction is determined by the motivation of the employees. Employees are motivated to the extent that they believe they will share in the success of their efforts. Management must effectively communicate with employees and provide them with the rewards, recognition, and empowerment needed to ensure continued progress. The elements of motivation must be continuously reviewed and improved by management to eliminate wasted time.

CATEGORY 3: CUSTOMER FOCUS

Customers and products belong in this category because they represent management's responsibility to continuously understand customers' needs and provide products that meet those needs. A customer focus keeps the business aware of the changes taking place in its environment and provides the knowledge needed to change the product or service. Figure 11.3 illustrates the customer focus improvement process.

Customers. Customers' needs are continuously changing through the advancement of technology. Businesses must utilize effective processes to allow them to monitor and prioritize customer needs and to define the needed products and services. These processes must be efficient so that employees do not spend too much time in the definition stage, continuously change the definition, or introduce the wrong product.

Products. The products must meet customer needs for quality, cost, and delivery. The business must also be responsive to the changes in customer needs caused by technology changes and delivery/economic changes. This requires that the business has processes that are high quality, low cost, and of short cycle times.

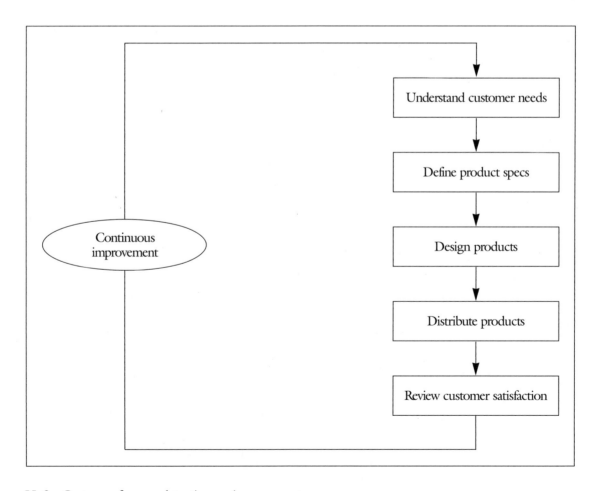

Figure 11.3. Customer focus and continuous improvement.

CATEGORY 4: TOTAL PARTICIPATION

Organization and teamwork are included in category 4 because they represent management's responsibility to synthesize all of the different processes and people in the business into a cohesive system focused around a common set of goals. Figure 11.4 represents the improvement process for total participation.

Organization. The organization must reflect the strategy of the business and provide the interfunctional relationships required to build cohesiveness of purpose and goals. The organizational relationships are the catalysts to synthesizing all of the different pieces of the business into a common system. In the absence of the proper structure, the functions of the business will work at cross purposes and drain the business of vital energy.

Teamwork. The organization needs the proper structure to be effective; at the same time, it needs individual employees to support one another within that structure. The organization is like a fisher's net, and people are the knots that hold it together. One weak link and the purpose is undermined. Management must ensure that the environment supports people working together as teams dedicated to a common purpose.

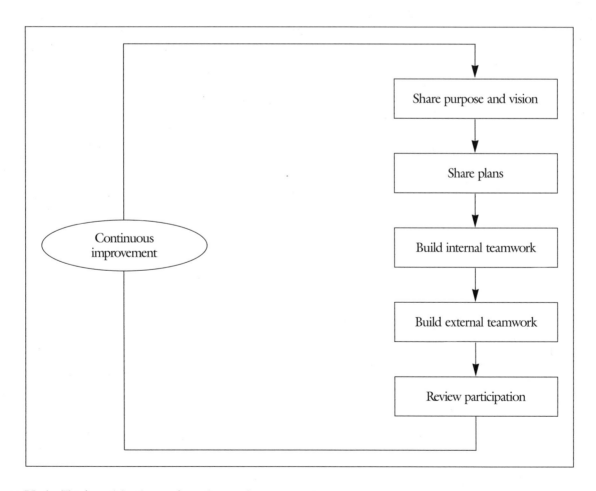

Figure 11.4. Total participation and continuous improvement.

CATEGORY 5: SYSTEMATIC ANALYSIS

Analysis and continuous process improvement belong in category 5 because they represent management's responsibility to analyze variation that is detected in the environment and within the business and provide consistent responses and improvement. Figure 11.5 illustrates the systematic analysis improvement process.

Analysis. The business needs a process to continuously analyze the changes in the business and the environment. The analysis process ensures that all deviations are appropriately considered and are responded to in a consistent manner. In the absence of a solid analysis process, the business will not be responsive to changes, and will thus become unable to compete in its environment. The method of analysis is the SQC of business.

Continuous process improvement. The information from the analysis of change must be used to modify the responsible processes in a manner that brings on continuous improvement. This process improvement methodology is the PDCA of business.

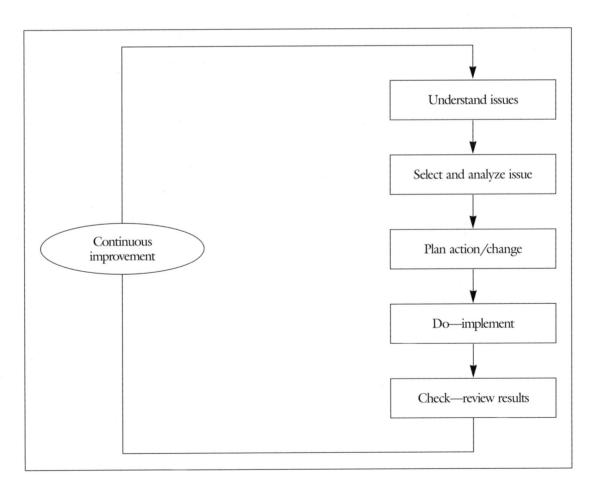

Figure 11.5. Systematic analysis for continuous improvement.

THE TOTAL QUALITY MANAGEMENT SYSTEM

The five TQM categories can be viewed as a total quality management system, as shown in Table 11.1. This single perspective not only shows the vertical relationships as previously defined, but also shows some interesting horizontal relationships. The top row, for example, identifies the functions of management that relate to understanding the business situation, defining needs, and planning for improvement; the middle row relates to the implementation of those plans; and the bottom row is the review and adjustment activity. This model represents a total quality management system.

There are different approaches available for managers to influence the effectiveness of the management system shown in Table 11.1 (Shores 1990). Some of these approaches are more effective than others. For example, in the first category under *values*, a business can choose to take a Theory X approach and set up an autocratic environment. Conversely, management can use a Theory Y approach and allow employees more individual discretion and decision-making authority. The choice a business makes will have a definite impact on the level of commitment and loyalty employees show toward the goals of the company. Some businesses may choose to offer significant amounts of training to their employees, while others may not; the outcome in quality and efficiency will be different for those that provide training and those that do not.

Another example is the planning element. Some businesses believe in highly structured planning systems that permeate the organization; others believe in generalizations that spread by word of mouth. In either case, the business that achieves the highest level of buy in and coordination of resources toward its goals will be the most successful.

In the customer focus category, some businesses use a highly structured process for analyzing and prioritizing customer needs, like quality function deployment; others do not. The business that has the least amount of wasted effort and best product fit in the market will be the most successful. In manufacturing the product, some use JIT processes and some do not. The business with the shortest cycle times, lowest cost, and best quality will be the most successful.

The WCM methods discussed in Tables 1.1, 1.2, and 1.3, represent some choices that managers have to improve the effectiveness of their management system and their subsequent business success. When these methods are viewed in the context of the management system shown in Table 11.1, a relationship to the management function provided can be seen. This is illustrated in Table 11.2. Where Table 11.1 is a generic management system that does not prescribe specific methods, Table 11.2 does.

Table 11.1. Total quality management system.

Management functions

Organization effectiveness	Management commitment	Leadership	Customer focus	Total participation	Systematic analysis	
Planning Set the direction of the business.	**Values** Establish a strong culture toward quality and customer satisfaction.	**Planning** Set visions, objectives, strategies, and measures for the entire organization.	**Customer needs** Evaluate and define customer needs into product specifications.	**Organizational links** Establish clear cross-functional linkages of goals, measures, and strategies.	**Understand issues** Do situation analysis to know if organization is meeting its vision.	Plan
Productivity Provide and use the resources efficiently.	**Investment** Provide training and capital investment to build a business.	**Motivation** Provide incentives, communication, and gain sharing to motivate quality and productivity.	**Product design** Design products and processes to meet customer needs.	**Teamwork** Provide structural tools—teams—to ensure everyone is involved.	**Continuous improvement** Use statistical methods to ensure that changes result in improvements.	Do
Adaptability Be flexible and responsive to needed changes in the environment.	**Organization review** Review the effectiveness of the values and investments, and make continuous improvements.	**Progress reviews** Review progress toward goals and make continuous improvement.	**Customer review** Review customer satisfaction and make continuous improvement of products and services.	**Team review** Review effectiveness of teams and involvement to make continuous improvements.	**Process review** Review the processes and method of improvement; make continuous improvements.	Check

→ Continuous improvement

Act

Table 11.2. WCM methods in the TQM system.

Management functions

Organization effectiveness	Management commitment	Leadership	Customer focus	Total participation	Systematic analysis (TQC)
Planning Setting the direction of the business	**Values** –Respect individual –Teamwork –Quality –Customer satisfaction	**Planning** –Hoshin –New seven tools	**Customer needs** –QFD –New seven tools	**Organizational links** –Hoshin –Cross-functional teams	**Understand issues** –Identify issues –Select issue –Analyze issue
Productivity Providing and using the resources efficiently	**Investment** –Training –Automation –CIM –JIT	**Motivation** –Knowledge/ skill-based pay –Gainsharing –Empowerment	**Product design** –QFD –DFM –CIM –JIT	**Teamwork** –Quality circles –Self-managed teams	**Continuous improvement** –PDCA –Kaizen –SDL/SPL –Seven tools –Poka Yoke
Adaptability Being flexible and responsive to needed changes in the environment	**Organization review** –Employee survey	**Progress reviews** –President's annual business review	**Customer review** –Customer satisfaction survey –Customer feedback system	**Team review** –Quality circle reviews –Employee survey –Team effectiveness ratings	**Process review** –Check results –Kaizen –Poka yoke

Plan

Do

Check

→ Continuous improvement

Act

In each of the improvement models shown thus far, there is a common element of review. The review is an assessment of the effectiveness of the tools being used to satisfy the need. As noted, some of these tools are more efficient than others. The TQM model requires managers to continuously review the effectiveness of their decisions in each of these elements and make changes to improve the elements.

SUMMARY

The management system presented here was conceived with the engineering principles used to manage all systems. Those principles are feedback, analysis, and control. Engineers use these principles to design control systems for automatic pilots on airplanes and boats, thermostats for homes, and many other applications. The business and its environment are also a system, and the principles extend just as readily to the management system.

The role of the management system is to ensure that the business is in better harmony with its customers' needs than its competitors are. The five areas of management discussed in this chapter provide for feedback, analysis, and control. By doing so, they ensure that quality, productivity, and flexibility are continuously improved. As a framework for improvement, the TQM system provides a logical order in which to reengineer the factory by applying WCM methods.

TRAINING

The training that is outlined in the previous illustrations presents an enormous challenge to WCM businesses. Thomas J. Watson Jr., of IBM, once said that employee training must increase in geometric proportion to the rate of technological change the company is going through (Watson 1963). Given the amount of new technology being introduced to the world-class business, managers must change their way of thinking about training. In this environment, the old saying that people are our most important asset becomes more than a slogan, it becomes a necessity.

Some organizations have responded to this need by changing the way they deliver training to employees. In the past, most companies provided basic-skills training for employees at the time they were hired. This training was supplemented by educational assistance programs that provided financial aid for employees to pursue classes at night school. Today, a few WCM companies are providing high-quality classroom training and self-paced learning right on the factory floor.

The factory floor learning at two divisions of Hewlett-Packard is facilitated by a learning resource center (LRC). The LRC occupies space on the periphery of the production floor and is staffed by a training coordinator and administrative support. The LRC is made up of a classroom that accommodates up to 30 people, and six individual learning cubicles, each about 75 square feet. Each learning cubicle is equipped with a VCR and monitor, a desk, and a personal computer connected to a local area network. The LRC has a library of video training courses, computer training courses, and other self-paced learning manuals.

The mission and vision of the LRC are shown. These statements were carefully developed by the LRC staff in conjunction with the manufacturing management team.

> Mission statement: Provide education, training, and resources to equip employees with the knowledge and skills needed to be effective in a WCM environment.

> Vision statement: By maintaining an educational investment in our employees, the business is able to attract and maintain a flexible and competitive workforce with the skills and knowledge to be efficient/effective at existing and new tasks. Managers are able to make workforce transition decisions based on comparing retraining costs with other transition methods. As a result, the workforce is a competitive advantage to the business.

Training consultants are partners with managers and employees to develop appropriate education and skill plans. Learning opportunities are readily accessible to managers and employees in convenient, easy-to-use delivery systems that address individual learning style. The most efficient and effective training is delivered on demand.

TYPES OF TRAINING

The LRC offers many forms of training to employees. The training is broken into two major categories: self-paced training and classroom training.

Self-Paced Training

Self-paced training is available for over 30 different classes. These classes come in a variety of media, including PC-based, video, and book form. All employees are eligible to use the self-paced material at their own convenience, which means the facilities are open 24 hours a day. A few examples of the types of self-paced training are available.

- How to use Microsoft Word: Word processing
- Executive Memo Maker: A computer word processing program
- Lotus 1-2-3: A computer spreadsheet program
- Assertiveness training for professionals
- Be prepared to speak: Making group presentations
- Getting things done: Time management
- Alge-Blaster: Basic algebra

- Self-esteem and peak performance
- Smart Tools: PC in plain English
- Speed Reader II

Classroom Training

Classroom training is taught to larger groups of employees as determined by demand. These classes and workshops typically run from 4 to 40 hours. Some examples are discussed here.

TQC training. Teams are trained in the elements of TQC. They receive their training weekly in one- to two-hour increments. Total training time is 12–18 hours. The team progresses through the entire TQC/kaizen improvement process, learning to use the tools as they go.

Process of Management (POM). All managers and supervisors are taught a company-developed course called POM. This class runs two to three days for managers and four to eight hours for nonmanagers. Employees are taught how to continuously improve their management process in a TQC methodology. The outline is as follows:

- Understand the situation: Subordinates are surveyed as to the effectiveness of their manager in several areas.
- Select an issue: Managers identify their weakest skills.
- Analyze the issue: Managers try to understand the cause.

In class, the managers learn to lead through a sequence of steps as shown previously in Figure 4.1.

1. Form the team.
2. Establish a purpose and direction.
3. Create a shared vision.
4. Develop shared plans.
5. Lead the course of action.
6. Evaluate the results and process.
7. Improve continuously.

In the shorter version of the POM class, nonmanagers learn to understand the functions and language of this process. The more knowledge they have of the management process, the easier it is to participate in the development of shared plans, visions, and purpose. These skills are also used by the self-managed work teams as they go about their daily business.

Working in groups. In a two- to three-day class, all employees are taught how to conduct efficient meetings, resolve issues quickly, prepare agendas, and reach consensus. This class is essential to the team effort.

Interact. In a two-day class, employees are taught to communicate effectively and interact with their peers and supervisors. They are taught how to resolve conflict and maintain good working relationships.

Math for SQC. Employees who need additional math training to understand the basics of SPC/SQC are taught general math and beginning algebra. This is a 40-hour class spread out over several weeks.

Managing Time. In a four- to eight-hour class, managers and employees are taught specific techniques to make the best use of their time. Subject matter includes the use of Day-Timers to keep track of meetings, meeting notes, and follow-up actions.

Kepner–Tregoe Problem Analysis. The Kepner–Tregoe course is administered to all employees to teach them to solve specific problems. It is used in conjunction with the TQC/kaizen methodology.

LEARNING CONTRACT

Learning contracts are used between supervisors and employees to ratify an agreement to pursue training. The supervisor and employee regularly review the type of training needed by the employee to progress in his or her job and become a more productive team member. When a need is identified that can be satisfied by a class or self-paced learning unit, a contract is written specifying the agreement, including such terms as the class name and length. When this contract is signed by both parties, the employee is free to use all the facilities in the LRC to achieve his or her goal.

TRAINING BENEFITS

The training that has been provided to employees at Hewlett-Packard has been the key to implementing self-managed teams, JIT, TQC, and the other WCM tools. Visitors to the Lake Stevens division of Hewlett-Packard, the first to implement the LRC concept, often comment that the production operation seems to run itself. The visitors are amazed that production workers know so much about the business and the processes; sometimes they find it difficult to know whether they are talking to a production worker or manager. In fact, the business does very much run itself. The few managers of that division find that their biggest roles are teaching and facilitating team activities.

SUMMARY

There are many interesting and new approaches to training developing around the country in response to the need for better-trained employees. Still, many companies are hesitant to make investments in their workers because of costs or downsizing efforts.

Yet, employee training may be the only hedge against rising wage rates and capital investments. Training broadens employees' skills and increases their management function in a team environment. All of the WCM methods described here require that every employee have significantly more training than most organizations have provided in the past. Regardless of how the training is delivered, WCM companies of the future will need to spend more money. A learning resource center may seem frivolous for some companies, but for others it is an essential part of their strategy.

ISO 9000

The worldwide attention being applied to the continual improvement of quality has created a desire among many countries and companies to set forth minimum standards for assuring quality of products and services. The International Organization for Standardization (ISO) thus created and approved the ISO 9000 standards. These standards (ISO 9001–9004) have been adopted by many companies and government agencies that require supplier companies to conform to the ISO 9000 standards as the minimum criteria for supplier selection. Companies that do not conform to the ISO 9000 standards are likely to find that they will not be able to sell into certain markets, thereby reducing their sales potential.

There are four sections in the ISO 9000 standards. The following discussion is intended only as an overview of the standards. More detailed information can be found by consulting the ISO 9000 standard documents.

The general intention of the ISO 9000 standards is to provide the basis of a quality system that attempts to assure the following principles (excerpted from the ISO standard).

- The organization should achieve and sustain the quality of the product or service produced so as to meet continually the purchaser's stated or implied needs.

- The organization should provide confidence to its own management that the intended quality is being achieved and sustained.

- The organization should provide confidence to the purchaser that the intended quality is being, or will be, achieved in the delivered product or service provided. When contractually required, this provision of confidence may involve agreed demonstration requirements.

ISO 9001

Quality systems—Model for quality assurance in design, development, production, installation, and servicing

The ISO 9001 standard is inclusive of the kind of requirements that would be imposed on a supplier who is designing, producing, and/or installing a product, most probably of custom design, and is controlled by the contractual relationship between the customer and supplier.

ISO 9002

Quality systems—Model for quality assurance in production and installation

The ISO 9002 standard is aimed at the quality system requirements for assuring the quality of products that are designed as off-the-shelf commercial items. In other words, the producer designs the product to the requirements of a general market and sells that product to many different customers with the manufacturer's specifications applied.

As there are no contractual requirements that pertain to the design of the off-the-shelf product, the ISO 9002 standard aims to set minimal standards for the quality assurance of the manufacturing processes. This will help ensure that each product meets minimum acceptable standards and that the variation from lot to lot or week to week will be minimized. In this way, an individual customer can be assured (within reasonable limits) that the next product off the line will be as good as the last. In effect, the customer should have some assurance that the quality will be consistent with the expectation set over time. ISO 9002 achieves its objective by setting forth standards of accountability for organization, inspection and verification, documentation, purchasing conformance to specification, and traceability.

ISO 9003

Quality systems—Model for quality assurance in final assembly and test

This standard is "for use when conformance to specified requirements is to be assured solely at final inspection and test." The text of the standard states that ISO 9003 is to be used when the contract between two parties requires demonstration of a supplier's capability to detect and control the disposition of any product non-conformity during final inspection and test.

The different standards in ISO 9000 are intended to be complementary and not viewed as alternatives. In the case of ISO 9003, it may be used complementary to 9001 and/or 9002; however, it may also find applicability when third parties are involved in the supply chain. For example, a manufacturer may produce a product for a system integrator who in turn combines the product with other products. The system integrator may not have any direct influence over the product suppliers except through 9001–9003. The end customer may desire to contractually require the system integrator to conform to ISO 9003.

ISO 9003 achieves its objectives by setting forth standards for sampling, testing, documenting, and handling of nonconformance items to assure the level of quality desired and contractually agreed to by the two parties.

ISO 9004

Quality management and quality system elements—guidelines

ISO 9004 sets forth guidelines for implementing a complete quality management system. The quality management system is, as discussed in this book, the approach and methods used to manage and improve the quality of all the business' processes toward higher levels of customer satisfaction.

ISO 9004 approaches its objective by setting forth principles for management, marketing, design, and production. It provides principles for developing quality plans and audits of the quality system. In many respects ISO 9004 is a shallow cut at prescribing a TQM system in the manner of the Malcolm Baldrige National Quality Award.

ISO 9000 SUMMARY

ISO 9001–9004 adequately set forth standards by which companies can attain a reasonable assurance of quality of design, manufacture, installation, and improvement. They do not prescribe a standard of excellence, nor were they intended to do so; rather, they set minimum acceptable standards for doing business in an international environment. Companies wishing to achieve higher standards of excellence should pursue the Malcolm Baldrige National Quality Award and/or other more rigorous TQM approaches.

The ISO 9000 standards are continuously reviewed and updated every five years. The next revision is in final review and should be due for release around mid-1994. For more information on ISO 9000 standards, write to the ASQC or ANSI.

American Society for Quality Control
611 East Wisconsin Avenue
P.O. Box 3005
Milwaukee, WI 53201-3005

American National Standards Institute
111 West 42nd Street
New York, NY 10036

MALCOLM BALDRIGE NATIONAL QUALITY AWARD

For many years U.S. industry floundered in the pursuit of excellence. Many of the attempts at TQM were ill-conceived and failed, leaving a wake of bad feelings. In recent years, however, much has changed, thanks in part to the Malcolm Baldrige National Quality Award (MBNQA).

The MBNQA was initiated in 1987 by President Ronald Reagan. The award was named in honor of Malcolm Baldrige, secretary of commerce to President Reagan, who prior to his death had contributed so much to the development of U.S. industry. The award was established to create a standard of excellence for U.S. companies to pursue, thereby improving their competitive position in international and domestic markets. The award is managed by the U.S. Department of Commerce, National Institute of Standards and Technology, in association with ASQC.

Since the first winners were announced in 1988, the interest and involvement in the award has grown steadily. In 1992 alone, more than 250,000 applications were distributed. The growth was precipitated by many factors, the most significant probably being the wide-scale national recognition accrued to the winners. Other factors include, of course, the expected productivity and sales gains to be derived from the process improvements necessary to win the award. In some cases, companies are required to pursue the award by their customers. Such is the case of the suppliers to Motorola, a 1988 winner who subsequently made it a requirement for its future suppliers to apply for the MBNQA within five years.

However, all is not good news for the winners of the award. The winners are obligated to open their doors to the world and show them how they manage their processes and their improvement methodologies. Winners are not required to divulge proprietary competitive information; however, the information provided must be open to competitors as well as noncompetitive companies and industries. This places a huge resource drain on the winning companies; people must be made available for leading tours, training material must be developed, and presenters must be available to travel to the many quality forums. Despite the less-appealing aspects of winning the award, many companies are still actively pursuing it. No doubt, the good outweighs the bad, and it would appear that the MBNQA will continue to motivate U.S. industry for many years to come.

THE AWARD

For more details on the award, consult the *Application Guidelines* booklet, available from the U.S. National Institute of Standards and Technology. The award application and guidelines are designed to serve as a guide for applicants and to provide a basis for self-assessment. Most of the applications distributed are to companies that wish to do an internal assessment. Most companies will do self-assessments and/or work with a quality consultant for several years before applying for the award.

Award Categories

There are three categories of the award: manufacturing companies, service companies, and small businesses. Two awards may be given in each category each year.

Award Examination and Scoring

Applicants are assigned points based on their achievements in seven categories.

1. Leadership		95
Senior executive leadership	45	
Management for quality	25	
Public responsibility and corporate citizenship	25	
2. Information and analysis		75
Scope and management of quality and performance data and information	15	
Competitive comparisons and benchmarking	20	
Analysis and uses of company-level data	40	

3. Strategic quality planning		60
Strategic quality and company performance planning process	35	
Quality and performance plans	25	
4. Human resource development and management		150
Human resource planning and management	20	
Employee involvement	40	
Employee education and training	40	
Employee performance and recognition measurement	25	
Employee well-being and satisfaction	25	
5. Management of process quality		140
Design and introduction of quality products and services	40	
Process management: product and service production and delivery process	35	
Process management: business process and support services	30	
Supplier quality	20	
Quality assessment	15	
6. Quality and operational results		180
Product and service quality results	70	
Company operational results	50	
Business process support service results	25	
Supplier quality results	35	
7. Customer focus and satisfaction		300
Customer expectations: current and future	35	
Customer relationship management	65	
Commitment to customers	15	
Customer satisfaction determination	30	
Customer satisfaction results	85	
Customer satisfaction comparison	70	
Total points		1000

THE APPLICATION

The application must be submitted by the deadline set forth in the guidelines. After the applications are received, they are judged by at least four examiners who are trained and familiar with the industry segment of the applying business. After a consensus review with a senior examiner, those companies who qualify are selected for site visits.

The site visit and verification are conducted by at least five members of the board of examiners including a senior examiner. During this site visit, a report is developed for the panel of judges. The panel of judges makes award recipient recommendations to the National Institute for Standards and Technology which, in turn, presents the recommendations to the secretary of commerce for award decisions. Previous awards were made by the president of the United States at a special presentation in Washington D.C. All applicants receive a feedback report after the awards.

SUMMARY

The MBNQA has proven to provide an excellent TQM framework for companies pursuing excellence in quality and competitiveness. While there has been a fair amount of controversy about the award and its value, none can argue against its effectiveness in providing a positive incentive for quality improvement in U.S. industry.

The award is not prescriptive in terms of the types of tools that must be used as discussed in earlier sections of this book; however, it does present a framework that provides for the economic improvement cycle discussed in Figure I.1. When all the businesses in U.S. industry begin to actively pursue the requirements of the MBNQA and utilize proven cost-effective methods, the U.S. economy and standard of living will be safe from international competition.

For more information on the MBNQA write to either the ASQC or NIST.

American Society for Quality Control
611 East Wisconsin Avenue
P.O. Box 3005
Milwaukee, WI 53201-3005

National Institute of Standards and Technology
Route 270 and Quince Orchard Road
Administration Building, Room A537
Gaithersburg, MD 20899

IMPLEMENTATION STRATEGY

This chapter provides some ideas about how to approach the reengineering strategy. The current factory must continue to provide revenue and profit while the reengineering effort progresses. All redesign efforts contain an element of risk, and extreme caution is necessary to avoid costly pitfalls. A well-thought-out strategy is the best insurance against failure.

Reengineering is a science in and of itself, and success requires the application of disciplined methods. Reengineering the factory, like reengineering a product, starts with the engineer's knowledge of the product and its intended purpose. Engineers must also know which of the new technologies are applicable to their product and understand the capabilities of the new technologies contrasted with those of the current methods. Lastly, they must know how to combine these technologies in the most efficient way to fulfill the purpose of their product.

In the context of reengineering the factory, managers must also start with an understanding of the performance of the business and its intended purpose. They must know which of these methods are most applicable to their industry and business. The managers must also know the capabilities of their current processes and the capabilities of the WCM technologies. Lastly, they must know how to combine them in the most efficient way.

Efficient implementation means eliminating wasted effort. It means doing things right the first time. Thus, consistent methods, careful analysis, and objective decision making (based on data, not emotions) are essential parts of the reengineering strategy. The method described here is a disciplined one of process analysis and improvement. It follows the format of USA–PDCA used in describing the WCM tools.

Because every company is different, there is no single formula that applies universally. Large companies require different approaches than small companies; electronic product technologies require different approaches than chemical technologies; and original equipment manufacturers require different strategies than contract manufacturers. To avoid digressing into too many different situations, the focus for these discussions is on those factors that are common to all businesses.

TOP-DOWN APPROACH

A major redesign of the factory is not possible without the involvement and commitment of the highest officer in the company. Plain and simple, if the CEO does not view a redesign as important enough to take full responsibility for the changes, they will not happen. The transition to WCM affects every part of the company, including the culture. Nobody in the company has the authority to make this happen except the CEO. Experience has proven that companies who start down this path without top management commitment run out of steam before the really important things happen.

Task 1: Form the Team

The CEO's first responsibility is to form the transition team. The members of this team are the top managers of the company. Some businesses have called this team the *quality council* or various other names. The title is unimportant as long as the team clearly understands its role. The team's responsibilities include

1. Leading the development of the transition strategy
2. Assuming and assigning appropriate responsibility for implementation
3. Committing the resources to make it happen
4. Providing the incentives for continued progress and eliminating disincentives
5. Reviewing progress along the way and recognizing and rewarding accomplishments

These activities should not be turned over to middle- or lower-level managers. The credibility of the senior managers in the company depends on firsthand experience in these methods. Delegating these responsibilities to lower levels of management causes the rest of the organization to view senior management's commitment as mere *lip service*. Consequently, the results may not live up to expectations.

The team's first task is to develop an understanding of the overall vision and purpose for the organization. The following questions relating to the purpose and vision are typical.

- What is the primary purpose of the business?
- Are we trying to win the Malcolm Baldrige National Quality Award?
- Do we want to achieve the highest level of customer satisfaction, growth, and profit in the industry?

At this stage, the team members must consider whether they have the technical expertise to be self-sustaining; that is, does the team possess enough knowledge of the WCM methods to develop a strategy? In the likely circumstance that they do not, they must send someone out for training and/or bring in outside experts as necessary. There is no substitute for experience. The best insurance against failure is to get someone who has successfully walked this path before. The person(s) selected for this role serves as teacher and facilitator for the rest of the team.

Task 2: Understand the Situation

A general assessment of the company's current situation determines a benchmark from which one can measure future improvements. The first assessment done by the senior transition team should not involve too many lower levels. The top managers probably have most of the knowledge they need to accomplish this task. The assessment may cover such areas as the following:

Values. Do company values support a world-class environment (that is, customer satisfaction, teamwork, individual respect, and so on)?

Investments. How much capital does the business have tied up? Where? For what? How much expense has the company set aside for training and training resources?

Planning. Is the planning system pervasive across the company? Has the business clearly defined the vision and key success metrics?

Motivation. Are appropriate reward structures in place to motivate WCM performance; that is, quality, teamwork, and continuous improvement? Are the communication systems in place to ensure broad understanding and support of future action?

Customer feedback. Are the company's customer satisfaction measures (quality, cost, and delivery) defined clearly?

Product design. Is data available and measured on the performance of individual products; that is, material cost, overhead cost, internal and external defects, and on-time delivery?

Organizational responsibilities. Does the team understand what each function's role is in implementing the WCM methods? Are specific skills available where they are needed? Who are the internal customers of the different processes? Are the performance measures in place to assess results?

Teamwork. Does the organization have an appreciation for team performance? Are the teams self-managed and rewarded for successes?

Analysis systems. Does the company use a common analysis method as in USA–PDCA? Are statistical tools commonly used in analysis and decision making at all levels of the organization?

While top management is asking these questions, it may be tempted to collect input from other employees. A survey is a good way to attain this information; however, there are two reasons why conducting such a survey too soon may be unproductive.

1. The managers can probably do a fairly complete job of answering the questions without distracting other employees in the organization.

2. Doing a survey before a plan is in place to respond to the employee concerns may create an expectation for too much change too soon, and thereby may create disappointments where previously there were none. In other words, top managers should be pretty clear on where they think they are and what they want to accomplish before involving the rest of the company.

It is important for top management to set realistic expectations about the time it takes to achieve WCM performance. The principle time factor is the organization's ability to learn and assimilate the new methods. The rule of thumb is that it takes more time to implement WCM strategies for large organizations and less time for small companies. Companies that have 25–30 employees can achieve significant results in less than a year. Larger organizations of 500 or more employees may take four to five years to see comparable results. The other variables that affect time are the dedication and commitment of resources, and the availability of technical expertise to resolve problems.

Task 3: Select the Issue

The preliminary assessment provides management with an objective view of the organization. The management team uses this assessment to select the major issues and set priorities. The senior managers probably have a subjective view of where the problems are. Using statistical data, however, is the only objective way to make decisions.

Basic housekeeping issues. Some elements of WCM strategy are essential to all businesses no matter what their situation. These are basic housekeeping chores that the executive transition team should address first.

- Values: After the executive team has reviewed the values of the business, it should make the necessary adjustments and ensure that they are broadly communicated and understood.

- Planning: The executive transition team must achieve consensus on the fundamental measures and goals. It must also set appropriate milestones. The goals and measures need to be broadly communicated.

- Systematic analysis: Every company needs to have a training program that teaches employees to use the USA–PDCA method and the basic seven tools. This should be part of the initial training and be propagated as fast as possible. Everyone, from the CEO down, needs to think about their approach to problem solving in the same language. This will avoid confusion and redundancy as the organization matures.

- Teams: All employees must be trained in the methods of effective teamwork, as discussed in chapter 5. The CEO's transition team is the first on the list. This team must ensure that an effective team structure is developed and deployed across the company.

- Communication and rewards: All employees need to know that there are going to be major changes in the culture of the business, and that these changes will require new behavior patterns. They need to understand that they will be rewarded for their participation and support and that they should not fear for their jobs.

Divergent strategies. These elements are common to all businesses. Additionally, there are other elements that are not so common. These include JIT, CIM, ATM, and so on. Strategies for these elements of WCM depend on the industry, outsourcing strategy, and the maturity achieved in applying the basic housekeeping tools. If the organization is not mature in teamwork and applying basic process analysis and improvement methodologies, it will probably be unsuccessful in applying the more technical aspects of WCM strategy. The following discussions provide some insight into some of the differences seen in different companies. The magnitude of each of these problems will have a major impact on the strategy.

Poor product producibility. In many small start-up companies the product design contributes to producibility problems. Often, the problem develops innocently as the entrepreneur conceives a new product idea, works diligently to bring it to market, and starts shipping it as soon as possible in order to generate much-needed revenue. Little problems are not a great concern during the start-up phase because there is enough time and expertise available to *tweak* each product to specifications.

The volumes eventually grow beyond prototype quantities if the product is successful in the market. By this time, new people have been hired, the original design engineer is busy working on something else, and the parts just don't go together as they did before. Now, it becomes necessary to go back to square one. The product design must be modified so that it can be efficiently manufactured in a repetitive process. The once-overlooked little problems became big producibility problems.

Poor product design quality is to production capacity as a square peg is to a round hole. A square peg requires 50 percent more area in the hole it is to pass through than its own area; similarly, poorly designed products require more production capacity to get them through the process. Thus, it becomes imperative that companies understand the source of producibility problems before determining the correct strategy to pursue. It may be necessary to correct poor product designs before going after improved manufacturing processes or material quality problems.

Cash flow and returns on assets. Many companies are finding that they can improve their cash flow and return on assets by working with contract manufacturers. For many technologies this is very practical because the contract manufacturers have already made the investment to develop WCM capability. Considering this option, questions to ask include

- Can I do this better than everybody else?

- Do I have some proprietary advantage by doing it?

- Is there a sufficient contract industry available to reliably meet my needs?

- Does the contract industry already possess world-class capability?

- What do I gain by trying to make my factory world-class when it's already available?

Companies often rationalize their manufacturing operations out of fear that the competitive edge is lost when buying from the same contractors as their competitors. However, these fears are unfounded after a manufacturing process technology matures to a commodity status. Processes such as plastic molding, sheet metal fabrication, and printed circuit card assembly are supported by enough WCM contractors to make them redundant in the factory of an original equipment manufacturer (OEM). OEMs must learn to rely on product innovation and product design for their major productivity improvements. One of the first steps in reengineering the factory is to eliminate nonessential processes.

Task 4: Analyze the Issues

The executive team should now have some idea about the issues and the potential magnitude of their effect on the company. The next step is to analyze the issues. For example, if product design quality is an issue, one must determine what resources are required to fix the current products. Further, one must decide if the future product life warrants the investment. Concurrently, what is required to ensure that future new products are correct at introduction must be determined.

Consider the following example of how a company with $125 million in revenues and 600 employees approached these issues (steps taken in order of implementation).

1. Implemented TQC concepts (four year process)
   Saved $2 million/year in warranty and internal defect costs
   Saved $2 million/year in material costs

2. Implemented JIT material flows (two year process)
   Saved $15 million in inventory investment
   Saved $1 million/year in overhead costs
   Reduced production cycle times to 1.5 days
   Reduced floor space requirement by 30 percent

3. Used part of above savings to invest in automation
   Saved $1 million/year in labor and overhead
   Reduced setup times/learning curves

4. Implemented factory/design CIM system
   Reduced new product introduction times 10:1
   Improved equipment utilization by 20 percent
   Improved production quality by 30 percent

5. Changed from quality teams to self-managed work teams
   Reduced management overhead by 60 percent
   Improved morale and job satisfaction

This company progressed through these five steps over a period of four years and saved about $7 million/year in costs and $20 million in capital/inventory investments. Concurrent with these steps there were other activities proceeding, including the development of a support system for self-managed teams (new reward systems, organizational redesign, and so on). Marketing was learning new ways to assess customer needs, and the design group was learning about QFD and computer-aided design (CAD) tools. All of the managers were eventually trained in new management methods.

There was considerable overlap in the steps as shown. The order reflects the focus that was given to each project. As the organization's focus moved from one project to the next, it could not neglect what had already been done; therefore, resources were required to continue to make improvements in a never-ending (kaizen) manner. Subsequently, the business sold its subassembly production operation to a contract manufacturer.

This raises another interesting question for many large companies. Some of them have manufacturing operations that are geographically dispersed. During tough times they invariably start talking about consolidation to improve productivity and utilization of assets. One company's managers recently consolidated three operations and, at the same time, implemented TQM and continuous-flow manufacturing. Shortly after they were finished, they decided that they would buy those subassemblies from a contract manufacturer. If they had decided this two years ago, they would have avoided considerable pain and expense.

The company in question had not analyzed all of the alternatives available. Why? The managers were too inwardly focused. They failed to see the trends of the industry and realize how practical it was to form a strategic partnership with a contract manufacturer. Such decisions are life-or-death for some companies; they cannot be taken lightly. All alternatives must be considered and analyzed.

It is tempting to say that the analysis stage is the most important part of this process. However, each stage of the implementation is important and none should be slighted.

Task 5: Plan the Actions

When analysis is complete it is time to plan the actions. At this stage the implementation plans take on their final and comprehensive form. Every function, team, and individual must know what actions are expected of them in the implementation. The executive transition team must complete a transition plan that spans all functions of the business. Goals and strategies, including priorities, need to be established for the entire business. These plans must be deployed across the lower levels of the organization in a hoshin-like manner to achieve consensus and support from the rest of the company.

Individual projects should have team plans developed to support their implementation. JIT material flows serve as an example. Who will be the champions—the production control department? Does it have the proper training and know-how to implement a JIT system for the business? What products or production lines will be implemented first? Have similar businesses that have already implemented JIT been visited and learned from? Will the team do an experiment on a small scale first, or do it all at once?

Probably the most important aspect of the plan is the people. All of the WCM methods result in improved productivity. As a result, some processes will not require as many people as they did before. Therefore, there must be a plan to retrain and redeploy the company's people. A successful JIT implementation will eliminate most of the production control department. Employees may stand in the way of JIT because they do not see how they will benefit from its implementation. They must be given the opportunity to be retrained.

There are four important points to consider in planning for these critical implementations.

1. Learn as much as possible from others who have done it
2. Involve everyone affected by the outcome
3. Have a contingency plan in case things go poorly
4. Plan, plan, plan, and then just do it

Task 6: Do the Implementation

The critical part of the implementation phase is employee support and consensus. The employees must feel some ownership for the results and not fear the outcome. The more support for consensus about the plan, the better the implementation will progress. Keep good records of how things go. Have plenty of technical resources standing by in case of emergencies. Do not start pointing fingers if things do not go as expected. Instead, get the team together and find solutions.

Task 7: Check the Results

Keep good statistical data on the implementation. The executive transition team should schedule regular reviews with the project teams to ensure that sufficient resources are available and that roadblocks are eliminated. When problems are detected, they should be acted upon at once.

Most companies have adopted some kind of a regular team review process. The team reviews are structured to focus on the team's approach to applying the tools discussed here. The presentation format and documentation closely follow the USA–PDCA format or something similar. Many companies use the storyboard approach for these reviews. The storyboard represents a designated format that follows the steps of the USA–PDCA process.

Task 8: Act and Adopt

After the reviews are completed, actions are assigned to the responsible team or individual to make the necessary adjustments. Where adjustments are not necessary, the procedures should be well documented as a record for future reference. Upon completion of step 8 it is time to cycle back and proceed to the next opportunity.

Celebration. The completion of a cycle or achievement of a major goal is always cause for celebration. All employees appreciate this kind of recognition, and it should not be overlooked.

SUMMARY

In this implementation guide we have progressed through the USA–PDCA cycle. This has been done to demonstrate that the cycle is fundamental to all businesses and that it is an effective tool to use for organization redesign. Reengineering the factory causes change to every process and person in the business. The factory redesign should be approached with the same disciplined methods used in other schools of engineering. Similarly, the results expected are the same: world-class products must be precise in the manner in which they meet customers needs, and the world-class business must be precise, productive, and flexible in meeting customers needs.

As stated earlier in this text, there is no single approach that will work for everyone. The general approach outlined in this chapter is an example of how one company successfully achieved WCM status. Every business and its environment are different, and adjustments need to be made to suit each case. TQC has been modified a thousand times over by as many companies; ATM and JIT are currently being revised by Toyota as economic conditions dictate. The successful company will recognize the need for these changes as they occur and make the necessary adjustments. This is the most important point of WCM: the winners will be the companies that perceive the needed changes first and adapt to them in the most timely and efficient manner; the losers will be the companies that continue to pursue things the same old way or implement changes by rote.

BIBLIOGRAPHY AND SUGGESTED READING

BIBLIOGRAPHY

Bemowski, K. "Three Electronics Firms Win 1991 Baldrige Award." *Quality Progress* 24 (November 1991): 39–41.

Deming, W. E. *Quality, Productivity, and Competitive Position.* Cambridge, Mass.: MIT Press, 1982.

Feigenbaum, A. V. *Total Quality Control.* 3d ed. New York: McGraw-Hill, 1991.

Goozner, M. "Japan in Big 3's Boat." *Chicago Tribune* 9 May 1993, p. 1.

Imai, M. *Kaizen: The Key to Japan's Competitive Success.* New York: Random House, 1986.

Ishikawa, K. *Guide to Quality Control.* Translated by the Asian Productivity Organization. Tokyo: Asian Productivity Organization, 1986.

Lawler, E. M. University of Southern California. Verbal presentation, 1987.

Mizuno, S. *Management for Quality Improvement: The 7 New QC Tools.* Cambridge, Mass.: Productivity Press, 1988.

Shores, A. R. *Survival of the Fittest: Total Quality Control and Management Evolution.* Milwaukee: ASQC Quality Press, 1988.

———., ed. *A TQM Approach to Manufacturing Excellence.* Milwaukee: ASQC Quality Press, 1990.

Sullivan, L. P. "Quality Function Deployment." In *A TQM Approach to Manufacturing Excellence,* edited by A. R. Shores, 265–279. Milwaukee: ASQC Quality Press, 1990.

Taguchi, G., and Y. Wu. *Introduction to Off-Line Quality Control.* Tokyo: Central Japan Quality Control Association, 1980.

Watson, T., Jr. *A Business and Its Beliefs.* New York: McGraw-Hill, 1963.

SUGGESTED READING

Akao, Y., ed. *Quality Function Deployment.* Cambridge, Mass.: Productivity Press, 1992.

Christopher, W. F., and C. G. Thor, eds. *Handbook for Productivity and Measurement.* Cambridge, Mass.: Productivity Press, 1993.

Ishikawa, K. *What Is Total Quality Control?* Translated by David J. Lu. Englewood Cliffs, N.J.: Prentice-Hall, 1985.

Juran, J. M., and F. M. Gryna, eds. *Juran's Quality Control Handbook.* 4th ed. New York: McGraw-Hill, 1988.

King, B. *Hoshin Planning.* Methuen, Mass.: GOAL/QPC, 1989.

Schoenberger, R. *Japanese Manufacturing Techniques.* New York: Free Press, 1982.

Stark, J. *Handbook for Manufacturing Automation and Integration.* New York: Auerbach Publishers, 1989.

INDEX